THE JESUS DIARIES

A Walk Through the Wilderness

BY JODI RAE BAILEY

Nicky~
GOD bless you as you
journey with Jesus through
the wilderness!
Jodi Rae Bailey

XULON
PRESS

DEDICATION

⁓ɞɞ⁓

My father, Donald Ray Clere, has experienced many of his own wilderness moments, yet he has always remained fixed on the Author and Perfecter of his faith. Throughout the desert wastelands of his life, he persevered, believed and never gave up hope. He has found what many lack—a satisfying relationship with Jesus Christ. Because of his devotion to the Lord, I visited the well and took a drink of water that has quenched my thirst. Like my father before me, there may be desert days ahead, but the Living Water that fills my soul springs up eternal life and brings me hope.

Thanks, Big D, for being strong in the desert, for standing up to temptations that destroyed weaker men, for trusting and believing in a God who walks with you through the wilderness. It is with great joy that I dedicate this book to you.

ACKNOWLEDGEMENTS

Jesus, thank You for walking in the wilderness for me. I am doing my very best to follow the footprints You left in the desert dust. Thank You for making my pathway straight. I love You with all of my heart.

My precious husband, Shay, thank you for your constant encouragement and support as I wrote this book. I praise God for you! Let us always look to the One who made it through the wilderness, and as we face desert days in our lives, may we always remember that He has gone before us. I love you, and I look forward to sharing the rest of this journey with you.

My family and friends, thank you for encouraging me. I pray that each one of you will cling to the life that Jesus offers to you through His saving grace. Thanks for being there for me during my moments in the wilderness. I love you all.

TABLE OF CONTENTS

_꒰ꓳ꒱_

INTRODUCTION

—ᘓᘔ—

Over the next forty days, you will journey with Jesus into the wilderness—into those days of intense testing—prior to the three years of His earthly ministry. What did He think about during those days? Did He wonder about His place in this world, the days of Creation, the great Fall? Was He amazed at how the grip of sin would be conquered? Did He face emotional and mental anguish as He thought about how religious men would reject Him and how His own family would call Him crazy? Did He feel the joy of victory when He concentrated on the fact that Satan and his allies—God's foes—would be crushed by the heel of His foot and death would be vanquished? What happened in those wilderness moments?

I want to take you on that journey with Jesus—a journey into the heart of wonderment—complete wonder at the things that Jesus experienced in the wild. The Bible does not hold a detailed account of what actually happened during those forty days and forty nights. Luke's account tells us, *"Jesus, full of the Holy Spirit, returned from the Jordan and was led by the Spirit in the desert, where for forty days he was tempted by the devil. He ate nothing during those days, and at the end of them he was hungry"* (4:1-2). Did Satan tempt Jesus incessantly during those forty days—walking with Him, watching Him, hovering over Him, observing Him—waiting for just the right moment to devour Jesus with a tempting word or thought? Did Satan have a strategic plan of attack?

Or, did Jesus experience forty days of fasting and then face the tempter? Did Satan wait until Jesus was overcome with hunger and human weakness before dangling the carrot of power in front of Him? Matthew's account tells us, *"Then Jesus was led by the Spirit into the desert to be tempted by the devil. After fasting for forty days and forty nights, he was hungry. The tempter came to him and said..."* (4:1-3a). What actually happened? Did Jesus spend time alone in the wilderness before He was approached by the devil? Or, was Satan a companion during Christ's entire stay in the wilderness? For example, Mark's account tells us, *"At once the Spirit sent him out into the desert, and he was in the desert forty days, being tempted by Satan"* (1:12). Is Mark suggesting that Satan was a constant presence around Jesus during those forty days? There are no answers for us. In fact, as the synoptic gospels are compared, they leave us with looming questions. There is no mention of fasting in Mark's particular account, and he is the only author to make mention of the wild animals Jesus may have encountered, *"He was with the wild animals, and angels attended him"* (1:12-13). What are we to make of Mark's rendition of the story? Did Jesus fast? If He was in the company of wild animals, was He in any danger? Did He have to face down any lions? And what about the angels mentioned in Mark 1:13? When did the angels attend to Jesus? Daily? At the end of the forty day experience?

The fine points of our Lord's encounter in the wilderness are left to wonder and speculation; however, we do hold to the notion that Jesus was tested, tempted, tried and prepared—just as the Israelites were tested during their forty years in the desert. Moses writes in Deuteronomy 8:2, *"Remember how the Lord your God led you all the way in the desert these forty years, to humble you and to test you in order to know what was in your heart, whether or not you would keep his commands."* Unfortunately, the Israelites—like all mankind—failed to keep God's commands. Jesus Christ, on the other hand, was the perfect example of faithfulness. He was tested and did not fail. He was tempted, and yet He did not succumb. Such loyalty to God's purposes guarantees that Christ has what it takes to be the Savior of the world; He passed the ultimate test of faithfulness in the wilderness and the ultimate test of obedience on the cross.

The Jesus Diaries gives you a glimpse of what it might have been like during those forty days—I want you to experience the wilderness with Christ as you read what might have been His thoughts, ideas and feelings. The forty diary entries will make you stop and think—you will be challenged to consider what really happened during those days of testing. You will begin to wonder what Jesus felt, how He ached, what He encountered and how He survived. And, as you ponder on the actual happenings of those unknown events, maybe you will begin to connect to the holy humanness of God. Maybe, for the first time ever, you will truly understand that God became man so that we could know Him. Maybe *The Jesus Diaries* will be an instrument of hope for you during the days when you are tested; knowing that a Greater One has gone before you.

And just maybe, when you grasp the fact that He felt hunger, cold, thirst, pain, loneliness; that He felt like you—then, you will whole-heartedly accept the idea that His suffering on the cross was real and genuine; that the pain of His sacrifice was felt with human hands and feet. Although Jesus was God incarnate—God made man—His place on the cross was not a creative performance; it was not "make believe" or imagined. Jesus was not a character in a God-directed play acting out a part; He was God as a man living out His holy, divine purpose—to bring salvation to the world.

Weeks in the wilderness prepared Jesus for His walk down the Via Dolorosa. He emerged from those days of testing with clarity and strength of purpose. Jesus was ready to fight sin and win; He was ready to face death and conquer. Our Lord was ready to carry the cross of Calvary.

I believe His days in the wilderness are as mysterious and miraculous as the power He displayed when He gave sight to the blind, health to the leper and legs to the lame. The testing He endured during those forty days prepared Him for the battle He would face before Satan—a battle He would win because of His sincere desire to please God, to obey God, to be God. He refused to live off of anything other than the holy word of God, He refused to worship anything other than the one true God, and He refused to test the heart of His Father, God.

Although I know no particular details about the Lord's days in the wilderness, Scripture leads me to believe that He prayed, He worshipped, He fellowshipped with God, and when He was tempted by Satan, He overcame evil with Truth. My imagination lets me gaze into the realm of wonder, animation and awe as I consider His thoughts, His feelings and His actions during those days of mystery. *The Jesus Diaries* is an inspirational work of possibilities, capturing what could be the actions of Jesus as He encounters creatures, inanimate objects and His tempter. The entries contain what could have been Christ's questions and thoughts throughout His forty day journey and some simple, yet profound responses from God. *The Jesus Diaries* is in no way an attempt to chronicle what actually happened to Jesus in the wilderness; it is a compilation of thought provoking ideas about our Savior's journey in the desert. One thing is for certain, all of the entries are written with one purpose in mind—to glorify the One who experienced the wilderness for us.

At the end of each daily *Diary* entry, you will find a short Bible study entitled, "A Day in the Desert." These studies will guide you to the scripture verses that inspired *The Jesus Diaries*. After reading the scripture verses, you will have an opportunity to record your own personal prayers or some thoughts about what you have read in the section titled "My Wilderness Moment." At the conclusion of the forty day experience, you will have a unique personal diary to serve as a testimony of your own journey through the wilderness.

The Jesus Diaries is an inspiration to me; a gift of my own amazement. For, I cannot even begin to understand why such a precious and perfect Lord would suffer physical pain and excruciating heartache for someone like me. I shudder to truly imagine what it was honestly like to know the prize of heaven and to surrender all of that glory, clothe Himself in human flesh and live on earth—all of that simply out of love for me...a selfish, prideful, unfaithful and ungrateful wretch of a being. When I consider the pain of His testing, the ache in His soul as He watched religion rule the hearts of men, the agony in His Spirit as He was abandoned by the God He loved, served and obeyed, I am overwhelmed. I am overpowered with a fierce love and loyalty for the One that I will never be able to repay. I am overcome with a sense of humility because of the position I have received through His death and resurrection. I am overjoyed at the promise that I will obtain an eternal place in a kingdom that my finite mind can only hope for and imagine. I do not understand—I never will; however, I trust and believe in Him.

These *Diaries* are a soul-fulfilling, heart-opening look into a God who did everything He could possibly do to make Himself completely accessible to those He loves. He became one of us so that we could know Him fully. There is no greater love than this.

I pray that you allow me the privilege of literary license as you walk with Jesus through His *Diaries*; for laced within the fictional geography of vivid imagination are Biblical accounts containing the mighty acts of a wonderful God and a blessed Savior. My prayer is that these *Diaries* will draw you to the Scriptures; and that as you ponder on the actions of Jesus Christ that you will draw nearer to the beautiful reality that you are adored and cherished by a great Lover who most likely thought of you during His days in the wilderness.

Jodi Rae Bailey

DAY 1: FATHER OF THE WILD

SCRIPTURE

Then Jesus came from Galilee to the Jordan to be baptized by John. But John tried to deter him saying, "I need to be baptized by you, and do you come to me?" Jesus replied, "Let it be so now; it is proper for us to do this to fulfill all righteousness." Then John consented. As soon as Jesus was baptized, he went up out of the water. At that moment heaven was opened, and he saw the Spirit of God descending like a dove and lighting on him. And a voice from heaven said, "This is my Son, whom I love; with him I am well pleased."

Matthew 3:13-17

JESUS PRAYS

Father of the Wild,

Why did the Spirit lead Me to the wilderness today? At times I find it a comfort to be alone and withdrawn; for it is in these times that I can deeply commune with You, but why now? It would seem a time to rejoice and celebrate, rather than a time to retreat. And yet now, here I sit in the desert alone.

My solitude deepens the reality of My brief time here and what I must do to fulfill the purpose ordained by Your hands. I know that My journey will not be easy. In fact, it will be wrought with much pain and suffering. Yet, I see past all of that—because I know those days are temporary and Your plan will prevail.

The moment before I entered the wilderness is etched into my heart; O, what joy I experienced in baptism. How beautiful were the feet of John the Baptist. His work is to be rewarded; for he prepared the way for My coming. I will never forget the look on his face when I asked him to baptize Me. His look was that of reverent fear and amazement mixed into one. Were the situation not so serious, I might have laughed at the time. For now, looking back on his countenance I cannot help but smile. John—such a dear cousin and believer. He trembled just a bit when he grasped My hand and shoulder. But, as he lowered Me into the water, I felt his strength and knew that he believed in a prophecy fulfilled.

Father, it was incredible to emerge from the water! My Spirit soared with a sense of victory. For I knew this baptism was a beautiful picture of the death and resurrection which will soon be revealed in My life. As the dove of Your Spirit descended from the heavens, My heart was flooded with such peace and comfort. How great it is to please You and to share in such glory.

The strength of Your voice as You declared me Your Son in whom You are well pleased brought such fulfillment to Me. O God, those gathered at the Jordan River were overwhelmed at Your presence. The expressions on their faces were priceless. O, how wonderful to know You; how marvelous to hear Your voice; how magnificent to watch others recognize You!

Dear Father, the work before Us is great and wonderful. I know this journey is just a beginning. I also know that at any moment I can leave this place. I can return to the home where I belong, and those in this place will be left to die. I do not have to suffer. I do not have to join in this divine plan. For I am heavenly. And yet, I want nothing other than those who dwell here to know My love, Your love; I want them to be captivated by the grace You offer. I want them to know the freedom found in forgiveness, and I know that freedom will cost Me dearly.

I am in this wilderness moment, ready to face the trials and temptations before Me but, I cannot bear this great test of faith without You. I know the tempter will come to Me as a companion during these days. Do not forsake Me. Guide Me, lead Me, help Me. I need Your strength; for the days will be long and wearisome. Let Me overcome. For the victory is Ours, and I long to bring Your children home to glory.

Here I sit in this desert alone, yet even in My solitude I celebrate.

Jesus

DAY 1: A DAY IN THE DESERT

Read Mark 1:12-13.

Immediately after Jesus was baptized, He entered the wilderness to begin a forty day journey full of tests, trials and temptations. I wonder what He was thinking. What must have been running through His mind?

Think of a wonderful occurrence in your life when you felt elated, when you were full of such joy and happiness—so much so that you just had to tell someone else about your experience. It may have been the birth of a child, the moment after a marriage proposal, the day you turned sixteen and passed your driving test, when you hit your first homerun. Can you remember the emotion? Do you remember who was with you to witness the experience? Do you remember who you called on the phone? How did you celebrate the event?

I remember the instant my husband proposed to me. It was so sweet, so amazing—a moment so full of precious joy! After the initial excitement, I looked at him and said, "What do we do now? Who can I call?" I wanted to share my news—to tell the world about my engagement. The excitement bubbled up inside of me, and I just could not contain it!

Imagine with me the scene of our Lord's baptism. The Bible tells us, *"As Jesus was coming up out of the water, he saw heaven being torn open and the Spirit descending on him like a dove. And a voice came from heaven: 'You are my Son, whom I love; with you I am well pleased'"* (Mark 1:10-11). I would venture to say that in the very moment when God proclaimed His love for Christ, when He claimed Him as His Son, when He declared His pleasure in Jesus—that our Lord was elated. The joy that filled His soul must have bubbled up inside of Him to a point where He felt unable to contain it! And yet, He did not go home and celebrate with His family. He did not travel to the next town and share His experience with friends and neighbors. Instead, the Bible tells us that Jesus Christ was sent into the desert. The Spirit of God led Jesus into a place of solitude, a place of loneliness, a place of testing and trials.

Can you fathom what it must have been like to move from a place of utter joy to a place of sheer and utter quiet? Christ was left alone, without any human contact. What about you? How has your life moved from moments of utter joy to sheer disappointment? One moment you are on cloud nine because you received a great sales commission, the next moment you are being told that the company needs to downsize and you are losing your job. One moment you are having a carefree lunch date with your girlfriends, the next moment your phone rings with news that your loved one has passed away. One moment you are celebrating your grandson's birthday, the next moment you are having your drug addicted daughter arrested. For this is the ebb and flow of life. We live inside both moments of joy and moments of pain. The comforting fact is that Jesus understands our situations. He knows what it feels like to celebrate one moment and to hurt the next. Our pain is not foreign to the Lord because He has experienced heartache as well.

In the desert, in moments of pain, loneliness and temptation, the Lord placed His hope and strength in the truth of God and His holy Word. We must follow His example so that we can overcome those moments in life when we feel like quitting, giving up and giving in.

Trust and believe that your life—the ups and the downs—are important to Jesus Christ, and He wants to be your companion and friend when your eyes are filled with tears of laughter and of pain. When your life shifts on a dime and moves from that moment of utter joy to unbearable pain—when you feel like you are in a desert with no one to talk to, to lean on, to hold onto—cry out to the One who hears.

DAY 1: MY MOMENT IN THE WILDERNESS

Think about a "desert" time in your life. Maybe you are in a desert situation today. Write a prayer asking God for the strength to overcome, or write some thoughts about today's Day in the Desert.

DAY 2: GOD OF THE SUFFERING

SCRIPTURE

The Spirit of the Sovereign Lord is on me, because the Lord has anointed me to preach good news to the poor. He has sent me to bind up the brokenhearted, to proclaim freedom for the captives and release from darkness for the prisoners, to proclaim the year of the Lord's favor and the day of vengeance of our God, to comfort all who mourn.

Isaiah 61:1-2

JESUS PRAYS

God of the Suffering,

Today You spoke to My heart and reminded Me that My suffering is not in vain. Yes, it seems odd that the Spirit led Me to the wilderness immediately after My baptism, but I understand. It seems logical that I would have stayed and celebrated with John and the other believers, but, I know You did not want Me to enter into the wilderness without first experiencing such a delightful and fulfilling moment. For, My heart is overflowing with joy, and My spirit is fully equipped for the encounter I will have within the next several weeks. For now, even though I find Myself in a place of solitude and quiet, I am ready.

I cannot imagine how it would have felt to be led to the wilderness before My baptism. I have entered here satisfied—the depths of My soul know the fullness of Your presence—and because of that awareness, I will survive this journey. For You are the strength of My life and My portion forever, and because You are in Me and I am in You, I will conquer these days of testing; I will stand strong against the adversary.

I wish that the suffering I shall face could be avoided—and yet to save man from his own evil bent, I must experience a pain beyond comprehension. Physically I shall be challenged, yet it shall pale in comparison to the mental anguish I will encounter. For over these forty days I shall hunger and thirst for more than mere bread and water—My Father, I shall ache for the souls of men and women. I shall be brokenhearted for those who refuse the love You offer. I will ache for companionship—especially when My mind is overcome with a sense of utter loneliness. But, I believe the truth that We are One—You shall always be with Me. In the midst of temptations I shall stand upon Your promises; I shall stand upon truth.

Yet, rest assured, My dear Father, that I will rejoice in the wilderness as well. For I shall see sights and hear sounds that will cause Me to rise up and shout "Glory to God in the highest." I shall be reminded that miracles do happen; I shall once again find peace in knowing that nothing is impossible with God. For with God, donkeys talk, seas part, ax heads float, lame walk, blind see and the dead live. Nothing, My Father, is impossible with You. And, during this wilderness journey, My body may grow weary, yet My spirit shall find strength for the days ahead. For I remember that You are enthroned above the circle of the earth. You stretch out the heavens like a canopy over Me (Isaiah 40:22).

I will not neglect to cherish the sights and sounds of the wilderness. I will lift My eyes and look to the heavens; look at the starry host one by one—for I know each star by name. And because of Your great power, not one of them is missing (Isaiah 40:26).

For even now the words of the prophet Isaiah speak to My heart: *"I took you from the ends of the earth, from its farthest corners I called you. I said, 'You are my servant'; I have chosen you and have not rejected you. So do not fear, for I am your God, I will strengthen you and help you; I will uphold you with my righteous right hand* (Isaiah 41:9-10).

> *"I have called you in righteousness; I will take hold of your hand. I will keep you and will make you to be a covenant for the people and a light for the Gentiles, to open eyes that are blind, to free captives from prison and to release from the dungeon those who sit in darkness.*
> *I am the Lord; that is my name!"* (Isaiah 42:6-7)

I know that You are with Me, Father God. I know that You will sustain Me and keep Me while I am here in this desert. And I will hold unswervingly to You and to the strength that comes from You. Through obedience, I will conquer; through Your Word I will overcome. For I am Your Son—in whom You can be well pleased!

Jesus

DAY 2: A DAY IN THE DESERT

Read Luke 4:14-21.

Do the verses sound familiar to those in Isaiah 42?

Read Isaiah 61:1-2.

In the book of Isaiah, the prophet was probably referring to himself as the servant God called to free the people from bondage and captivity; however, on that day in the synagogue, when Jesus read Isaiah 61:1-2 from the scrolls, He indeed fulfilled a prophecy from God. Jesus had absolutely no doubt that His mission on earth was to preach the good news, proclaim freedom for the prisoners, give sight to the blind, release the oppressed and proclaim the year of the Lord's favor. Jesus busied Himself traveling from town to town in order to tell others about the love of God—a message that would free people from the bondage and captivity of sin and all of its deathly consequences.

Maybe, just maybe, when Jesus was in the wilderness God gave Him a glimpse of the days ahead. Maybe, just maybe, God had a heart to heart talk with our Lord—encouraging Him to endure because a day was coming when He would stand before a multitude of people in a nearby synagogue and read these words from the prophet Isaiah:

> *The Spirit of the Sovereign Lord is on me, because the Lord has anointed me to preach good news to the poor. He has sent me to bind up the brokenhearted, to proclaim freedom for the captives and release from darkness for the prisoners, to proclaim the year of the Lord's favor and the day of vengeance of our God, to comfort all who mourn* (Isaiah 61:1-2).

I don't know. Of course I am simply speculating, but maybe when Jesus was in the wilderness, God said something like, "Jesus, when the prophet Isaiah spoke those words he was talking about You and all that You would do during Your earthly ministry."

And, I can only imagine that on that day in the synagogue when Jesus read those words from Isaiah that His Spirit did a somersault inside His being. I can only imagine that the fulfillment of the prophecy sent a surge of power through Jesus that set the rhythm of His heart into overdrive.

So many times when I read the Bible, I have a tendency to read the stories in such a matter-of-fact manner; however, I would venture to say that Jesus was nowhere near as boring as I make Him out to be. In fact, I think He was quite the opposite. For, on that day when He read those words from Isaiah, I would like to imagine that it thrilled His soul—that He was so overwhelmed with joy that He welcomed the idea of sitting down (as was custom when one taught in the synagogue) because His knees grew weak with the utter excitement of it all.

And, I would like to imagine that God the Father threw back His head and laughed a hearty laugh—one of pure joy—at the fact that His plan, bit by bit, was playing itself out in the lives of people. And that His Son, the One who weathered a wilderness journey, now sat in a synagogue as the living fulfillment of a prophecy spoken many years before His time on earth.

When, if ever, have you been so thrilled and excited at something God has done in your life? Is your relationship with God boring, distant and calculated? Or, are you so overwhelmed at His hand in your life that your spirit turns somersaults? Have you forgotten that God has called you to righteousness? Have you overlooked the fact that you, too, are a servant of the Lord, and that God promises to hold you with His hand? There is absolutely nothing that you will ever face alone—because God is there to keep you. Just as Isaiah and Jesus were commissioned to be lights to the Gentiles, to open the eyes of the blind—so are we. Let us live our lives in such a way that we too fulfill God's desire to free captives from the prison of sin.

DAY 2: MY MOMENT IN THE WILDERNESS

What is going on in your relationship with God today? Are you doing somersaults because of the excitement His love brings into your life, or is there a sense of distance between you and God today? Honestly evaluate your relationship with God today, and then write a prayer or some thoughts about today's Day in the Desert.

DAY 3: A NEW THING

GOD SPEAKS

Jesus,

See, I am doing a new thing! Now it springs up; do You not perceive it? I am making a way in the desert and streams in the wasteland.

God

DAY 3: A DAY IN THE DESERT

Sometimes when we pray, we expect God to answer in long diatribes. Sometimes we want dissertations to help us understand why He is allowing something to happen. We sometimes long for paragraphs; yet we only receive a few words.

Throughout the *Diaries* you will notice that God's responses to Jesus are short and sweet words of Scripture. In our own personal lives, God speaks to us in various ways; however, He usually chooses to speak to our hearts and our minds through the pages of His Holy Word. At times, we might find meaning in several chapters of the Word, and other times, we may find the encouragement we seek in just a few precious verses. Sometimes God responds to us with simple, one word answers. But, He always responds. And although His responses are not always what we expect, they are always wise, good and right.

We need not neglect taking time to read the Bible, for within its chapters and verse is food for the hungry soul and water for the thirsty spirit. In this life we cannot survive without divine nourishment. Let's not starve our hearts and minds of the good fruit of God's Word.

Read Isaiah 43:19.

Isaiah is writing about the deliverance and restoration of Israel, God's chosen people. He writes with excitement and anticipation as he reveals the words the Lord has spoken, *"See, I am doing a new thing! Now it springs up; do you not perceive it? I am making a way in the desert and streams in the wasteland"* (Isaiah 43:19). Although the nation of Israel has been unfaithful, God has shown mercy upon the people and has promised to redeem them.

Jesus Christ is that Redeemer. And, we can rest assured that He was our "way in the desert." Even though, after leaving the desert and beginning His earthly ministry, the world would not recognize Jesus as the Messiah, even though He would be mocked, beaten and crucified, God had a plan—to do a new thing! God would do away with the former things—the sins of our past—and He would make a way for us to have a personal relationship with Him through the forgiveness of our sins. That "new thing" God was talking about? Well, that was a new life that He has offered to us because of His enormous love and amazing mercy!

As Jesus physically endured the heat and agony of a desert wasteland, I wonder if He found encouragement in a few precious words that God may have spoken to Him. I wonder if He was reminded of the fact that He was a "stream in the wasteland" springing up to do a new thing!

DAY 3: MY MOMENT IN THE WILDERNESS

God is always doing new things in our lives. Sometimes we just do not take the time to recognize His work around us. What new things are happening to you today? Write a prayer or some thoughts about today's Day in the Desert.

DAY 4: THE GREAT I AM

SCRIPTURE

He said to me, "It is done. I am the Alpha and the Omega, the Beginning and the End. To him who is thirsty I will give to drink without cost from the spring of the water of life."

Revelation 21:6

JESUS PRAYS

The Great I AM,

The desert floor on which I stand seems to stretch into eternity. As I look to My right and to My left, I see no beginning and no end. This vast array of wilderness reminds Me of who I AM. My presence cannot be contained within the confines of time or space. In all creation there is no one like Me; no man, no creature, no being. May the power of the Almighty assist Me now as I wander in this endless desert.

Today I am strong, yet I know that in the days before Me My body will grow weak and weary. Lead Me not astray, but deliver Me from the evil one who taunts Me even now with his presence. He is like a gnat that needs to be crushed; a troublesome irritation — deceived into believing that he is in a position of greatness, yet he remains weak. My mere presence here causes him great strife; he is planning and scheming—ever so watchful of My movements. He is waiting to attack; trying so desperately to overcome a Power beyond his grasp. He will fail. Though Satan accompany Me now, he will be vanquished—he will be blotted out, snuffed out—destroyed. For, no weapon formed against Me will stand because I AM. I AM a royal Son; a Son of David. I AM a Wonderful Counselor, the Mighty God, the Everlasting Father, the Prince of Peace.

These days in the wilderness are My days of final preparation; those days of testing before I embark on My public ministry—a ministry of justice and righteousness formed before time itself—a government of grace and peace with no end; the fulfillment of a Davidic reign.

Opposition will arise. Great minds will challenge Me in the days ahead; as the Tempter will challenge Me in these next weeks. But Your zeal will prevail. Your purposes will not be thwarted. The Lord Almighty, the Great I AM, will accomplish that which He set out to do from the Beginning.

Provide Me with a wilderness of thought—a vast Beginning and End; an Alpha and Omega—to Your greatness and power. Nothing and no one can overcome He who is mighty and strong.

And, when this work is finished I will stand before the heavenly nation, the counsel of the godly. I will look to My right and to My left, and I will see no beginning and no end. I will hear the thunderous applause and the roar of Hallelujahs to I AM. Then, I will sit in that place of glory, as I have before—as You do now—and as We will forevermore. For just like this desert wilderness, there will be no end to our eternal reign.

Jesus

DAY 4: A DAY IN THE DESERT

If you have never been to a desert, you may have seen pictures or viewed desert scenes from a movie. Does it not look infinite? It seems as though the desert stretches for countless miles with no beginning and no end. I wonder how it must have felt to Jesus— knowing that He was in a place so immeasurable, so boundless.

Maybe it was a physical reminder of who He is. Maybe it was a tangible statement on the fact that God is the great I AM—immeasurable, infinite, boundless, eternal.

Our human minds are unable to grasp the truth—we are unable to calculate in our heads the mathematical miracle of infinity—time without end. And, that is why our faith is so important. Hebrews 11:1 says, *"Now faith is being sure of what we hope for and certain of what we do not see."* It is our faith that allows us to trust and believe that God has always been—that He is the Alpha and Omega, the Beginning and the End.

And, our faith leads us to believe that Jesus is the Messiah—that He is who He claims. In the book of John, we read how Jesus connects Himself with God, the great I AM of the Old Testament. In John 6:35, Jesus says, *"I am the bread of life. He who comes to me will never go hungry, and he who believes in me will never be thirsty."* He defines Himself in this manner six other times throughout the gospel of John, each time revealing the same idea—He is the only way that we will ever know God, the only way that we will ever experience eternal life.

Read the following verses and write down the description Jesus gives of Himself:

John 8:12 and John 9:5
John 10:7,9
John 10: 11,14
John 11:25
John 14:6
John 15:1,5

In each of these passages, Jesus identifies Himself as the great I AM of the New Testament, reminding us once again that He and the Father are One. We see Him as the light of the world; the gate; the good shepherd; the resurrection and the life; the way, the truth and the life; and the true vine.

Do you know Jesus Christ? Have you ever believed by faith that He truly is the Son of God, and that He really is the gateway to heaven? Are you in a living relationship with the Resurrection and the Life? Have you experienced the True Vine?

Jesus loves you, and He is *the bread that came down from heaven* (John 6:41). The time that Jesus spent in the wilderness is not a fable; it really did happen. It probably did not happen exactly the way *The Jesus Diaries* portrays, but it did happen. Jesus Christ is God made man, and He did come to earth to die for all of our sins. The Lord suffered on a cross for all of us so that we can have eternal life. John 6:46-48 says, *"No one has seen the Father except the one who is from God; only he has seen the Father. I tell you the truth, he who believes has everlasting life. I am the bread of life."*

Read Romans 10:9-11.

If, in this very moment, this is the first time you have actually believed in your heart that Jesus is Lord, then I rejoice with you in your decision to place your faith in Christ. Please be sure to tell someone about your decision—you may want to visit your local church or talk to a family member. I encourage you to find a friend who can help you learn ways to study the Bible and pray.

DAY 4: MY MOMENT IN THE WILDERNESS

Write a prayer of confession to God or some thoughts about today's Day in the Desert.

DAY 5: THE FIRST AND THE LAST

GOD SPEAKS

Jesus,

I am the first and I am the last.

God

DAY 5: A DAY IN THE DESERT

Read Isaiah 44:6-8.

I do not know about you, but I absolutely enjoy these verses! I appreciate the fact that I have a God who does not back down from His claims; He is not afraid to challenge others with the Truth. He does not fear close scrutiny because He knows that no one will be able to stand against Him—that no one else will be able to usurp His authority. God knows that counterfeit gods will be cast, created, forged; yet none will stand the test of eternity—for God is the "first" and the "last"—and "there is no other Rock."

My husband is a funny character; he loves competitive sports and takes joy in the thrill of pushing himself to succeed. He often says, "I don't mind a cocky competitor if he can actually back up his claims."

I mean no disrespect at all when I say that God can back up what He claims! He is not just puffing into the wind—He is not building Himself up to be a great God...only to disappoint us in the end. He is God! The real thing! The only true God. He will not fail.

Maybe, just maybe, as Jesus was living out His days in the wilderness, God reminded Him of His position...His place...that there is no other God! And, maybe, just maybe God's *"Who then is like me? Let him proclaim it"* was a challenge to the tempter.

Satan cannot back up what he claims! He is just puffing into the wind—building himself up to be a great god...only to disappoint and disillusion in the end. He is not God! And, he will fail!

I believe that in those wilderness moments, Jesus lived on the beautiful Truth that there is no god apart from God! I believe that He found the strength to endure because He knew what was yet to come...He knew that Israel's King and Redeemer, the Lord Almighty, would prevail.

Take a few moments to evaluate your life. Have you forged any other gods in your life? Is God Almighty taking a back seat to your career, your physical fitness, your dating life? Are you more concerned about your meticulously manicured lawn than time spent reading God's Word? Do you worship God, or do you worship the image you see each morning in the mirror? Who is really God in your life? Do you dare stand before God and hear Him challenge you with the words, *"Who then is like me? Let him proclaim it"*?

DAY 5: MY MOMENT IN THE WILDERNESS

Does an honest evaluation of your life reveal that you are bowing down to other gods in your life? Write a prayer asking God to help you put Him first in your life, or write some thoughts about today's Day in the Desert.

DAY 6: CREATOR GOD

SCRIPTURE

And God said, "Let there be lights in the expanse of the sky to separate the day from the night, and let them serve as signs to mark seasons and days and years, and let them be lights in the expanse of the sky to give light on the earth." And it was so. God made two great lights—the greater light to govern the day and the lesser light to govern the night. He also made the stars. God set them in the expanse of the sky to give light on the earth, to govern the day and the night, and to separate light from darkness. And God saw that it was good.

Genesis 1:14-18

JESUS PRAYS

Creator God,

Last night I lay awake counting the stars that dotted such a deep midnight. I was reminded of moments before we knew stars—the moments when there was nothingness. Amazing—what a word can do, is it not? For in one tiny breath, the void was filled with celestial beings providing light and depth of space. You created the heavens. You are God; the One who fashioned and made the earth.

You founded it! You did not create it to be empty, but formed it to be inhabited. You are the Lord, and there is no other.

The sun has just begun to reveal itself. My head still rests upon a mound of sand. I am tired in body, yet My Spirit rejoices as darkness gives way to the light of a new day. The greatness of Your world is immeasurable; Your creation is beautiful. What does this earthly dominion have to offer? It offers nothing that does not already belong to the Holy One. My enemy holds the keys to a kingdom that was given to him by the hand of the Creator; his power does not match that of the Almighty—for he did not create. He only rules that which he is allowed to rule; yet, indeed, he rules. He is ruler over that which is wicked and dark; apart from the Light and absent of Truth. Why would I lower My sights to his limited dominion? For light and darkness cannot mix. The light shines in the darkness, and the darkness retreats. Like the stars upon which I gazed last night, I am that glimmer of hope and light in this ever-so-darkened world. I will shine; I will bring light and depth to the lives of many. My allegiance will not be turned; for I have been with the One who created light—I have seen the light of glory, and darkness will not persuade Me.

As he hovers on a nearby rock, the darkness enshrouds him. I can barley look upon him; for the sin disgusts Me; I can feel the hairs on My arms and neck rise. Yet, the time is not nigh; I will not destroy him in this wilderness—the battle with sin will not end in this moment—for it is not time to abolish his reign forever. I must conquer death to redeem the ones We love, and that time has not yet come—but it will. His darkness may follow Me and inhabit the wild home in which I dwell thus now; however, he will never overshadow the Light.

Jesus

DAY 6: A DAY IN THE DESERT

Like me, you may not have been afraid of the dark when you were a child. Truly, my fear of the dark did not rear its head until I became an adolescent. And, even then, it wasn't necessarily the "dark" that I feared, it was what I imagined happening in the dark that scared me. In fact, as a single adult there were many times when I slept with a light on—it just seemed to comfort me throughout the dark night—I felt that my bedside lamp chased away all evil; allowing me to actually sleep in peace. Admittedly so, there are times even now—when my husband travels—that I will sleep with a light (or two) on throughout the house. There just seems to be a sense of security in the light—and rightly so.

For, truly there is a peace in the Light of Jesus Christ.

Read the following verses and write what you learn about the Light:

> **2 Samuel 22:29**
> **Psalm 18:28**
> **Psalm 27:1**

From these verses we learn that God is our light, and He turns our darkness into light. We do not need to fear anyone or anything because we can be secure; knowing that we are safe inside God's love.

Read Psalm 119:105.

What does the Bible tell us about God's Word? God's Word is a light for our paths! We do not have to travel in darkness because we have the Word of God with us! As we read it, our hearts and minds are enlightened, and we gain more knowledge and insight as to the depth of God's love for all of us!

Maybe Jesus did lie on His back in the wilderness and count the stars one night—or on many nights. Maybe He did remember the Creation moment and how amazing it was to watch the black expanse fill up with the sun and moon separating darkness from light. Maybe He smiled remembering what it was like to watch as the sky as it was dotted with numerous, brilliant stars.

And, Jesus is that light for us. Life with Him means that we are separated from a life of sin and darkness and we have entered into a life of light and wonder and awe. He is the Light of my life!

DAY 6: MY MOMENT IN THE WILDERNESS

Take a few moments to think about your life before you knew Jesus Christ. How has He given "light" and life to you? How has your life been separated from darkness? Write a prayer or some thoughts about today's Day in the Desert.

DAY 7: MAKER OF ALL THINGS

GOD SPEAKS

My Son,

I am the LORD, who has made all things, who alone stretched out the heavens, who spread out the earth by Myself.

God

DAY 7: A DAY IN THE DESERT

When I was a child, my younger brother and I would make what we called "hideouts." We had a ping-pong table in our basement, and we would gather sheets, blankets, sleeping bags and pillows and set to work. Our first task was to spread all of the sheets and blankets over the ping-pong table, being sure to drape them over the sides of the table and down onto the floor. After creating our makeshift tent, we would fill it with pillows, our sleeping bags and toys galore. We could spend hours playing in that special man-made hideout.

Read Psalm 104:2, Isaiah 40:22 and Isaiah 44:24.

The Bible tells us that God stretches out the heavens like a tent or a canopy. In fact, God spread out the earth by Himself. Amazing!

I know I probably could have made that childhood, makeshift tent alone; however, it was much easier with my younger brother's assistance. Spreading out all of the sheets and blankets with another set of hands to help me stretch, pull and straighten the "tent" was quite helpful. Even now, as an adult, when I put a clean set of sheets on the bed, it is a task I can do alone; however, it sure is a lot easier when my husband lends a hand. And yet, God's Word tells us that He alone "stretches out the heavens like a canopy." God alone created all that we see. The earth below us and the heavens above us; He placed the sky as a canopy over us—and as I gaze above I stand amazed. For, just as the desert probably seemed endless in scope to Jesus, the sky seems endless to me. What a comfort to know that God alone placed that blanket above my head and created a tent for me! And, as in the days of my fun and fulfilling childhood, God wants me to have hours and hours of endless joy as I "hideout" in His canopy of love.

How often do you "hideout" with God? When is the last time that you have taken a few hours or even a few minutes to spend time with God?

Today, take a moment to just gaze at the sky. Or, tonight sit and watch the sun set. Gaze at the vast horizon and stand in wonder and awe at our Creator. You may choose to sit under a canopy of stars tonight as you remember that God alone stretched out the heavens.

DAY 7: MY MOMENT IN THE WILDERNESS

Are you "hiding out" with God, safe in His protection, or are you venturing out on your own? Write a prayer or some thoughts about today's Day in the Desert.

DAY 8: GOD THE POTTER

SCRIPTURE

Then God said, "Let us make man in our image, in our likeness, and let them rule over the fish of the sea and the birds of the air, over the livestock, over all the earth, and over all the creatures that move along the ground."

So God created man in his own image, in the image of God he created him; male and female he created them.

God blessed them and said to them, "Be fruitful and increase in number; fill the earth and subdue it. Rule over the fish of the sea and the birds of the air and over every living creature that moves on the ground."

The Lord God formed the man from the dust of the ground and breathed into his nostrils the breath of life, and the man became a living being.

Genesis 1:26-30

JESUS PRAYS

God the Potter,

Sand from the desert trickles through My fingers as I sift handfuls of dirt from one palm to another. Precisely how long have I been sitting here? Minutes feel like hours; hours like minutes in My dirt-filled abode.

But, this dust; O, this beautiful dust. It takes Me back to a day so long ago—the sound of Your voice still echoes in My ears. I can still hear You say, *"Let us make man in our image, in our likeness"* (Genesis 1:26). How amazing and wonderful to form man from the dust of the ground; just like this simple dust within My hands.

To watch as You scooped handfuls of dust from the earth and shaped, molded and fashioned a human vessel of clay was a miraculous sight. O, the wonder of being; the awe of existence. Heaven refused to breathe as We watched You fill Adam's nostrils with the breath of life. What a beautiful creature—dust made to clay and brought to life.

I, too, have been made with this dust. As Job proclaimed, *"I too have been taken from clay"* (Job 33:6). You knew that the Messiah would inhabit a bodily form. You knew that I would be born into this vessel of clay to be used for Your noble purpose—to bring the gift of salvation to all mankind. For by laying aside glory and taking on the nature of human likeness, I have stepped into a dusty cloak of skin and shelter of bones; a tabernacle that houses within its being the Spirit of the Living God. My flesh, like man's, is malleable; however, to his impressions I will not form. My will is compliant only to the beat of My Father's heart, and I will not bend to the enemy. O, that man could fully embrace the reality of my humanness; that he could grasp the fact that My human death is his birth canal to life eternal.

Will he ever understand? Or has he forgotten that You are the Great Artist; that You are the Almighty Potter? Has man turned things so upside down that he thinks the Potter is like clay? *"Shall what is formed say to him who formed it, 'He did not make me'? Can the pot say of the potter, 'He knows nothing'?"* (Isaiah 29:16) Does man really believe that he can be God? Is he so deceived in his heart that he thinks he is more powerful than the One who designed his very being? *"Does the ax raise itself above him who swings it, or the saw boast against him who uses it? As if a rod were to wield him who lifts it up, or a club brandish him who is not wood"* (Isaiah 10:15). Man is not greater than his Maker, and yet he tries to deter-mine the steps of his life. Has he grown wiser than God? *"For the foolishness of God is wiser than man's wisdom, and the weakness of God is stronger than man's strength"* (1 Corinthians 1:25). Does he trust in his goodness, his morality, his benevolence? Can he save himself? *"As for man, his days are like grass, he flourishes like a flower of the field; the wind blows over it and it is gone and its place remembers it no more"* (Psalm 103:15-16). *"O Lord, what is man that you care for him, the son of man that you think of him? Man is like a breath; his days are like a fleeting shadow"* (Psalm 144:3-4). *"Cursed is the one who trusts in man, who depends on flesh for his strength and whose heart turns away from the Lord. He will be like a bush in the wastelands; he will not see prosperity when it comes. He will dwell in the parched places of the desert, in a salt land where no one lives"* (Jeremiah 17:5-6).

The reality of it makes Me weep; My dust-filled hands now brush the tears from My cheeks—a small amount of clay fills My palms. For that is the reason I left My place in glory—to redeem the clay pots You made; to fill the earthen jars with treasure from heaven; to bring life, healing, redemption. Do not toss these vessels into the potsherd—into the heap of useless, broken pottery pieces. Instead, use this Perfect Mound of Clay and fashion Me into a pot large enough to hold the sins of the world; large enough to hold the piles and piles of shattered, destroyed, hopeless earthenware pieces—and allow Me to make something beautiful from the dust and ash of man's mistakes. As in those days of old when You breathed into the nostrils of man and gave him life; exhale now into the depths of who I am and give Me sustenance—for the Inner Man is greater than My fleshly covering, and My Spirit will prevail. For although I dwell in this clay pot, I and the Potter are one.

Jesus

DAY 8: A DAY IN THE DESERT

I thank God that there could have been a day in the desert when Jesus played in the sand! I thank Jesus that there could have been a day when He wept over my mistakes and the sin in my life! I praise the Lord that He did not throw me away into a pile of broken pots, but instead He gave His life for me that I might know the joy of heaven. It is amazing! Who am I that God would actually care about me? And who are you?

Read 1 Peter 2:9.

As Christians we are chosen, royal, holy—we belong to God! In spite of our shortcomings and folly, we are loved and cherished.

Read Isaiah 64:8.

You are clay in the Master's hand. Are you allowing Him to shape your life, or do you have things turned upside down—and you are instructing the Constructor? Who is designing the days and moments of your life—you or the Great Architect?

Read 1 Corinthians 1:25.

Have you deceived yourself into believing that you know more than your Maker? That you are wiser than God? In what ways have you allowed your pride to direct the steps of your life rather than allowing God to give you direction? Are you managing God, or are you allowing God to manage and control your life?

Is your life a heap of broken pottery pieces, or are you a vessel useful to the Master?

DAY 8: MY MOMENT IN THE WILDERNESS

Who is controlling your life today—you or God? Are the pieces of your life lying in a pile of rubble, or are you allowing the Lord to shape you into a useful servant? Write a prayer or some thoughts about today's Day in the Desert.

DAY 9: GOD OF GRACE

SCRIPTURE

Then the eyes of both of them were opened, and they
realized they were naked; so they sewed fig leaves together
and made coverings for themselves.
Then the man and his wife heard the sound of the Lord
God as he was walking in the garden in the cool of the day, and
they hid from the Lord God among the trees of the garden.
The Lord God made garments of skin for Adam and his
wife and clothed them.

Genesis 3:7-8, 21

JESUS PRAYS

God of Grace,

The sun makes its way above the horizon today, and I am aroused
from My sleep. The rock upon which I slept last night is now a
pillow for two; for bathing beside Me in a ray of light is a reptile. He
basks without fear; his outstretched body forming a thick, leathery
line. I stare at him, amazed that something so seemingly serene is a
cause of enmity between he and mankind.

I arise and leave My resting place, My body feeling tired, yet
I have slumbered throughout the night. I want to move about this
land; to allow My body to stretch and awaken.

As I walk in the cool of the day, My thoughts are turned to that morning in the Garden; the morning that man and his wife hid from God. The weight of the shame they felt balanced with the sadness in Your soul. Upon tasting the fruit, they were aware of their nakedness; innocence was lost. And You knew at that moment what I know now—a sacrifice of blood must be made. For, to hide their nakedness and shame, an animal was slain; his skin becoming an instrument of grace—I am such covering.

A blanket for My bareness I do not need, for I wear the glory and righteousness of God. My exposure and vulnerability before You make Me not uncomfortable, and nakedness will not reduce Me to shame. For unlike the first man, I am aware of good and evil. I need not eat fruit from a tree to be like God, for I am God—no wisdom is needed other than that which I know comes from You. As in that morning long ago, when You cloaked Adam and his mate with the skins of animals, You will use Me as a covering for this world. For sin entered the world through the son of man, and that sin will be vanquished by the Son of Man.

Long before You walked in the Garden that morning, You knew the relationship had been broken; You knew the enemy had succeeded in striking his prey. Even so, Your compassion removed guilt and clothed the man and his wife with the warmth of mercy. The craftiness of the serpent that led that first couple to sin is no less powerful in this place. He slithers through this wilderness in hopes to lead Me astray. His only desire is to deceive Me, but I will not be disgraced. Waiting to strike, My enemy snakes his way around Me. He wants to entwine his evil motives into the depths of My heart so that I will waiver. His schemes coil beneath Me ready to collide with My obedience and poison Your plan. But I will not allow him to attack My heel; for, indeed, he will be crushed.

The snake once upon My pillow now slithers along My path; he leaves a cloud of dust around him as he meanders nearer to My feet. He knows not the limit of his power; for My heel is not his victory but his woe.

Jesus

DAY 9: A DAY IN THE DESERT

There are many reasons why my older brother is my hero, one being that he rescued me from a snake. I will never forget that day. It was a nice summer afternoon, and as usual, I was barefoot. When I walked out into our driveway, a snake was lying comfortably in a crack between two slabs of concrete. I screamed so loud that my brother heard me from his bedroom, which was located in the back of our home. He came running outside, and I am sure he expected to find me in a life and death situation. When he opened the back door, I was standing in the street screaming, "Snake, snake, snake" as I frantically pointed to the garage. You see, when I screamed, I gave the snake such a fright that he scurried into the garage for cover; therefore, I ran into the street! My heroic brother captured the snake, and as far as I was concerned, saved my life. He still laughs to this day about the time a harmless, garden snake scared me.

Well, I can say one thing for certain—if I woke up and a snake was lying on my pillow basking in the sun, I wouldn't stick around long enough to stare at him!

Read Genesis 3:13-15.

These verses reveal to us that the woman, Eve, blames the serpent for her behavior. We have heard it said, many times in a joking format, "The devil made me do it." Well, Eve was basically using that line of reasoning with God when she proclaimed, *"The serpent deceived me, and I ate"* (Genesis 3:13).

God then placed a curse upon the serpent—he would crawl on his belly and eat dust for the rest of his life. Hostility, or enmity, was then placed between the woman and the serpent. Yet, God being true to His gracious nature, made a way for that hostility to end—the day when Jesus Christ would crush Satan with the heel of His foot.

Read Romans 16:17-20.

In this passage, Paul is urging the Christians in Rome to protect their minds from smooth talk and flattery which can deceive. Does this sound familiar to Genesis 3? Eve definitely fell prey to the smooth talking serpent; yet, she made the choice to sin. Paul says, *"Be wise about what is good, and innocent about what is evil"* (Romans 16:19). He did not want his fellow brothers and sisters to entertain the false teaching of those who were not serving the Lord; he knew it would lead to their demise. In fact, Paul says, *"Keep away from them"* (Romans 16:17).

In Romans 16:20 Paul makes reference to Satan's final doom—similar to the serpent's demise in Genesis 3. Jesus defeated death when He was resurrected! He made a way for all of us to keep away from evil, and through His death on the cross all of us—although cursed by the weight of sin—have now been offered forgiveness for our sins and life eternal!

There will be a day when Jesus Christ will crush Satan under His feet once and for all!

DAY 9: MY MOMENT IN THE WILDERNESS

Have you become a victim to the smooth-talking serpent? Are you allowing the enemy to deceive you? Write a prayer asking the Lord to protect your mind and to help you keep away from evil, or write some thoughts about today's Day in the Desert.

DAY 10: MY HUMBLE GOD

SCRIPTURE

*The Lord sustains the humble but casts the wicked to the
ground.*

Psalm 147:6

JESUS PRAYS

My Humble God,

As I bow in this dusty terrain to pray, I remember the pride that
stood before You on the day that Satan was cast from Your
Presence. I will forever remember how it pained My heart to see an
angel struggle to assume authority and dominion over Jehovah God.
And, although I longed for that beautiful angel to rid himself of his
thirst for power, I knew that the decision had been made. And those
that followed Satan lost their position in Your kingdom as well.

So, although the tempter will follow Me and strike at My heels,
he shall be destroyed. For I know that a time is coming when Satan
and his demons will be crushed. His utter rebellion is something that
You will not tolerate. I know that the humble shall be sustained, yet
Your enemy, once a beautiful light, will be cast to the ground.

I rise from My place of prayer, My movement stirring the dirt
beneath Me. As I walk in this wilderness with strength and power,

the enemy slithers behind Me tasting the dust of My footsteps. I will not allow him to trip Me up—for as he wiggles around through My feet, he longs to deter My path. Oh, how he wants to twist himself around My ankles and drag Me down to his level. Yet, I walk in majesty knowing that the dust he eats is the taste of death. For the curse You spoke upon him long ago still remains: *"Cursed are you above all the livestock and all the wild animals! You will crawl on your belly and you will eat dust all the days of your life. And I will put enmity between you and the woman, and between your offspring and hers; he will crush your head, and you will strike his heel"* (Genesis 3:14-15).

As You said to Joshua, You now speak unto Me, *"I will give You every place where You set Your foot"* (Joshua 1:3). You are watching over Me, and You will not let My foot slip! For You are the Lord My God, and You will keep My foot from being snared! And, as I shake the dirt from My sandaled feet, I shall remove the enemy from My pathway. He will not gain a foothold over Me. As I walk this desert road, I will not swerve to the right or the left. I will keep My heart focused on the victory ahead, and keep My foot from evil. I will not lose sight—for the day is coming when I will sit at Your right hand—when You will make My enemy a footstool for My feet. He shall be crushed, and I shall be exalted—for I am holy and all people will worship at My footstool (Psalm 99:5; 100:1).

Jesus

DAY 10: A DAY IN THE DESERT

As our enemy waits to strike our heels, God reminds us that we are victorious! Because of what Christ has done for us, we, too, can crush the enemy with our feet. The enemy becomes our footstool rather than a foothold in our lives.

Are you turning to the right and to the left, or are you walking the path of life God intended for you? Does Satan have a grip around your ankles, dragging you down, holding you back from truly chasing after an intimate relationship with God?

Read Psalm 147:6.

How many of us in our pride will be *"cast to the ground?"* Think for a moment about the things in your life that are twisted around your feet hindering your freedom to walk undeterred. Bitterness? Are you angry at your spouse because your needs are not met? Excessive drinking? Selfishness? Are you too consumed with things that satisfy you—no matter the cost? Jobs? Busy schedules? Fear of losing control over your life? An unhealthy relationship?

These things can deter us from living the life that God so desires for all of us. If we are not careful with the way we walk—with the way we live our lives—then we will trip and fall.

Read Luke 10:1; 17-20.

Jesus sent seventy-two disciples into every town He was about to enter, and He asked them to pray and to tell those in the towns that the kingdom of God was near. The disciples did as they were commanded and came back to see Jesus. Upon their return, they were elated that even the demons would submit to them.

Of course the seventy-two had every reason to be overcome with joy at all they had seen God do and at all they experienced on their journey. However, Jesus wanted to remind them that He had seen Satan fall from heaven, and that he had given the disciples the power to trample on snakes and scorpions and to overcome the enemy—

but that the greatest joy should come from knowing that their names were written in heaven.

The enemy, Satan, will be destroyed. We can rest assured of that fact. God has also given us the power to conquer the enemy. However, we need to be careful to rejoice, not in our power, but in the fact that God has blessed us with salvation.

Read Revelation 20.

One day Satan will be destroyed completely—but let us not wait until his doom to be rid of him. Let us humble ourselves before God and watch how swift our feet will move towards a path of peace, joy and purpose.

DAY 10: MY MOMENT IN THE WILDERNESS

On which path are you today—a path towards peace, joy and purpose, or a path of prideful living? Write a prayer or some thoughts about today's Day in the Desert.

DAY 11: EVERY KNEE WILL BOW

_GÐ eᲒ_

GOD SPEAKS

Jesus,

Before Me every knee will bow; by Me every tongue will swear.

God

DAY 11: A DAY IN THE DESERT

Today, as I think about all of the suffering Jesus went through for me, I am amazed! Do you ever stop and think about the steps He took towards us, so that the gap our sin created would be filled? He exchanged places with us, so that we could experience forgiveness! He did not have to do this for us. At any given moment, Jesus could have left the wilderness. No armed guard held Him prisoner; yet, He was a captive of the love He has for us, so He finished His course—all the way to the cross. He made a choice to leave glory so that we could experience glory.

Think about something with me: Who among us would exchange places with a homeless person? How many of us would give up our warm, dry, safe shelters to live out on the streets? How many of us would do something so drastic just so another human being could have a better life?

Read Philippians 2:5-11.

Did you catch the essence of these verses? Jesus Christ, who being in very nature God, traded His position in heaven for a temporary home on earth. He was made in human likeness—to die on a cross for us! He traded His life for your life and mine! So that those of us without a home—a heavenly home—could become Kingdom dwellers.

Read Isaiah 45:23.

We have a reason to bow down and proclaim that God is God. The *Diaries* portrays Jesus bowing down in the dusty desert and praying to the Father. As we study the New Testament we see several instances when Jesus went off alone and prayed. I believe that it is safe to assume that Jesus fellowshipped with God through prayer and conversation while He was in the wilderness. And, even if He didn't bow down in the dirt, one thing is for certain—we should! Jesus is to be praised for who He is and for all that He has done for us! One day, every knee will bow and every tongue will confess that Jesus is Lord! Believers and non-believers will all recognize that the name of Jesus has been exalted above all other names! And yet, we do not have to wait until a distant, future day! Today, we can bow before our Savior and give Him honor for His faithfulness during the wilderness, His honesty during a mock trial, His steadfast obedience during beatings and torture, His sacrifice on the cross, His death-defeating resurrection and His glorious return! He deserves all praise and honor! To God be the glory!

DAY 11: MY MOMENT IN THE WILDERNESS

Are you bowing down in the dirt today? Write a prayer thanking Jesus for all that He has done for you, or write some thoughts about today's Day in the Desert.

DAY 12: GOD MY ROCK

SCRIPTURE

The Lord is my rock, my fortress and my deliverer; my God is my rock, in whom I take refuge. He is my shield and the horn of my salvation, my stronghold.

Psalm 18:2

"Because he loves me," says the Lord, "I will rescue him; I will protect him, for he acknowledges my name. He will call upon me, and I will answer him; I will be with him in trouble, I will deliver him and honor him. With long life will I satisfy him and show him my salvation."

Psalm 91:14-16

JESUS PRAYS

God My Rock,

Today My body is void of food, but I am filled with Your satisfying presence. Basking in the warmth of the morning sun, I stretch upon the stones that served as My resting place last night. Across from Me the coney also sun bathe; the young rest comfortably on the backs of their elders. Others playfully chase one another as some look for food. Were it not for this fast, I would share a meal with them.

The coney, this tiny creature of Yours, possesses a natural wisdom, for he finds a hiding place between the crevices of these rocks. He need not burrow into the ground for the tiny, cave-like spaces provide adequate safety. I am reminded of the Psalmist's words, *"The crags are a refuge for the coneys"* (Psalm 104:18).

Such smart little characters, although so very shy. I watch them without moving from My place of rest; for I know if I make a slight movement they will scurry back into seclusion in order to flee from assumed danger. The young I can hold within the palm of My hand; its elder is not much larger. As the writer of Proverbs once said, *"Coneys are creatures of little power, yet they make their home in the crags"* (Proverbs 30:26).

These little beings are amazing; each one fitted with the means for survival. The bottoms of its feet are clad with suction cups; helping him run on stone surfaces in order to flee predators. You supplied rocky fortresses as a dwelling place in which each colony of coney may shelter. Their tiny frames fit perfectly inside each crag, as if the crevice was specifically carved for them. For when the eagle circles above in search of sustenance, he will not find these critters who take refuge in this rock. Nor will the leopards find nourishment when the coney is within its hiding place; for inside the rock is complete safety.

I, too, am a rock—a rock of safety, a place to hide. For I am the Rock upon which You will build Your church. No evil that comes against Me will prevail.

As the coney finds a crag in a rock, Your children will run to Me, and I will save them because I am the perfect hiding place. When evil circles around them or pursues them, they will run to Me, and I will cover them. Your precious creation will dwell in the security of My love.

For as I can hold the young coney in the palm of My hand, I, too, will hold the hand of Your young. I will open My life before them so that they may find shelter in the crag of this Rock. From evil I will be their escape. From harm I will be their protection. In Me they will find haven from the storms of life.

They, too, are a powerless creature—for they are weak and frail and bent to sin. But, I will be their Refuge—if, indeed, they use the means for survival You have given—eyes to see the Way, ears to hear the Truth, hearts to receive the Life—and a Rock in which to hide. Let them run to Me.

I rise to begin My day and the coney take notice; they scurry into the home You have so graciously provided. I look above; an eagle circles. Today, however, he will not feast upon these little animals. For My presence has driven them into the harbor of safety You designed and they are safe inside the Rock.

Jesus

DAY 12: A DAY IN THE DESERT

My husband plays on a softball team in the town where we live. One particular evening, my parents and I decided to attend a game. We found the perfect spot for our lounge chairs. Just as we sat down, a huge dark cloud covered the field; rain was imminent. I ran to the parking lot to get the car for my aging parents. After they were tucked inside the car safe from the storm, I raced to retrieve our lounge chairs. Although I had an umbrella, it was no match for the whipping wind and rain. In mere seconds I was sopping wet! I knew my efforts to battle this storm were futile, and a burst of uncontrollable laughter came over me. There I stood, drenched from head to toe, laughing hysterically. I looked over at my parents, sitting in the car—warm, dry, safe from the storm—and they, too, were overcome with laughter.

Don't you wish we could learn to laugh more; especially when faced with the storms of life? But, many times, instead of remembering that we can run to the Rock for safety and shelter, we panic.

Read Proverbs 18:10 and Psalm 91:2.

Do you trust the Lord? Do you really believe that He will protect you and help you in your time of need? Or do you rely on your own strength? When troubles come your way, do you spend your time running around in a state of panic and fear, or do you run to Jesus? Do you see trials as opportunities for joy because you know that God has provided a hiding place for you safe inside His love?

Take time now to think about how you respond when the whipping wind and rain come your way. Are you in the middle of a storm today? Remember, Jesus has the power to calm the wind! He can and will take care of you. Don't try to battle the storms on your own. Instead, run to the Rock, Jesus Christ.

DAY 12: MY MOMENT IN THE WILDERNESS

Do you need to run to the Rock, Jesus Christ, today? Write a prayer or some thoughts about today's Day in the Desert.

DAY 13: HAVE YOU NOT HEARD?

GOD SPEAKS

Jesus,

Do You not know? Have You not heard? I am the everlasting God, the Creator of the ends of the earth. I will not grow tired or weary, and My understanding no one can fathom. I give strength to the weary and increase the power of the weak. Those that hope in the Lord will renew their strength. They will soar on wings like eagles; they will run and not grow weary, they will walk and not be faint.

God

DAY 13: A DAY IN THE DESERT

Not too long ago I was watching some television coverage of a triathlon. One particular racer had completed both the swim and biking sections of the race and now she was on the final stretch of a 26.2 mile marathon. One minute she was running and the next minute her knees were buckling, like that of a newborn calf trying to walk for the first time. Her legs were unable to sustain her. She would take a few steps, fall and then get right back up and start again. Watching her struggle was heart wrenching. Her body was exhausted, but she refused to quit.

All of us understand what it feels like to be weary. For, all of us, at one time or another, for one reason or another, have experienced emotional, mental, physical and spiritual exhaustion. So many times we try to accomplish too many things in too little time, and we wear ourselves out. On some occasions we push ourselves to the limit because we want more—bigger houses, nicer cars and finer clothes. We strive for the promotion to make more money so that we can have more things. Men feel the pressure to provide for themselves and their families. Women in the work place feel the pressure to keep the "anything men can do women can do better" mantra alive and well. Parents struggle to keep their children in private schools, extra curricular activities and the latest name brand pair of jeans. Teenagers juggle homework, chores, part-time jobs, church activities, sports and dating relationships.

We face a lot of demands each day of our lives. Some of us thrive under pressure. Some of us stress out when our plate becomes too full. Some of us know how to manage the many aspects of our lives. But, no matter what, all of us get tired. Life is full of fun and a lot of joy, but life can be a lot of hard work too.

Newborn babies are precious, but we lose a lot of sleep because they demand a lot of attention. Toddlers are so cute and curious, but we lose a lot of weight chasing them around as we try to keep them from pulling bookshelves down onto their heads. Teenagers keep us up at night, while we hope and pray they make it home close to curfew and in one piece. Spouses are wonderful support systems and they make the best friends, yet our marriages take a lot of hard work.

Are you relating to any of this? Sometimes, we can grow so weary that our knees buckle beneath us, and we are unable to carry the weight of our lives.

Do you ever wonder if Jesus grew so totally exhausted in the desert that He could barely walk? I do. I wonder what He felt like physically. I wonder if there were days that He was hot and ached for shade. I wonder if there were days when His body would not let Him take another step. Whether He fasted for a complete forty days or fasted various times while in the wilderness is not completely clear; however, the accounts in Matthew and Luke tell us that after forty days, Jesus was hungry. I know that my body grows weak and tired when I do not eat. I wonder what happened to Jesus. Were there ever moments when His knees buckled beneath Him?

One thing I can say with certainty is this: No matter the circumstances, whether He was physically exhausted and hungry or not, Jesus relied on God's Word during times of testing and temptation.

Read Isaiah 40:28-31.

Isn't it great to know that God tells us He will not grow tired or weary? He is strong, and we can depend on His strength. The Bible promises us that when we put our hope in the Lord, our strength will be renewed. We will soar, run and walk, and we will not grow weary or faint!

Sometimes it is hard to take a step back in order to evaluate our lives. At times we are so wrapped up in the busyness of our commitments and responsibilities that we forget to trust God, rely on God and put our hope in God.

Today, you might feel like you are so tired that you can't take another step. Or, you may have become so burdened with life that you have already stumbled; you have already fallen. Don't quit. Take God at His Word. Isaiah 40:31 says, *"But those who hope in the Lord will renew their strength."* Allow the Lord to renew you today!

DAY 13: MY MOMENT IN THE WILDERNESS

Are you placing your hope in God today? Write a prayer asking God to renew you today, or write some thoughts about today's Day in the Desert.

DAY 14: GOD OF ETERNAL PRESENCE

_⸻ ☙☙ ⸻_

SCRIPTURE

Enoch walked with God; then he was no more, because God took him away.

Genesis 5:24

JESUS PRAYS

God of Eternal Presence,

The days run together now. As I walk through the wilderness, My lack of food leaves a sense of emptiness; but Your presence seems to grow stronger each moment. I know I have so much more to experience here—for I must walk among Your people and show them a true expression of God's love. Yet, My heart still yearns for the glorious presence of home. Oh how wonderful to take this next step and find Myself at the right hand of the Father—much like Enoch (the one who was and then was no more). For how joyful he felt when his path crossed into the realm of heaven. How his steps quickened when he realized the street upon which he walked. To leap, to skip, to run in glory—oh how I long for such! It pains Me that there is no other way. For I know that when My foot finds its next resting place I will still be in this dusty region—this wilderness—away from the home I know and love. I welcome the day when I, like Enoch, will be taken away and carried back into My holy dwelling. For I, too, will jump and skip and run through the Kingdom—celebrating that I am once again in My rightful place. I am ever so homesick for that which is pure and right; such longing drives Me into Your presence and makes our communion My eternal home. Do not leave Me or forsake Me; for I cannot weather this wilderness walk without You.

The one who walks with Me now thinks he troubles My soul. He walks beside Me, his footsteps in sync with My very own. No matter his rhythm, he will never know Your presence as he did in days of old; he will never again commune with You in glory. He will only succeed in stirring the dust beneath his feet, but his path will never lead to the heavenly lands. For unlike Enoch, he walks with God in hopes to trip Me, in hopes to change the course of My path, in hopes to deter Me. But I will not change course. I will follow the path that You illumine with Your lamp and Your light. I will remain true to Your Word. For I am the Word; the Word made flesh. And, I will not twist or alter the pathway to Calvary. I go there willingly because I love the world.

Yet, this battle must wait for a distant appointed time. I cannot put an end to the enemy's treacherous ways here and now. But soon I will stop him in his tracks—terminate him; that he may walk no longer. How precious it is to know that he will one day be no more—he will neither walk nor skip nor run. His steps will be put asunder, and he will have no power to lead men astray; to turn them to the left or the right. His journey will end in death.

I walk in this wilderness to lead all men down a path of righteousness. This walk will not show Me mercy or grace; I will stumble under the weight of My cross, but I will bear it gladly. For, I will walk from this wilderness into the hearts of men from nations far and wide. My walk is the way to life; may many follow the footsteps I will leave.

Jesus

DAY 14: A DAY IN THE DESERT

Jesus. Jesus. Jesus. What a sweet name, Jesus. Say it out loud. The name above all names. God with us. God in our presence. God on earth. Jesus.

I am so grateful that Jesus walked in the wilderness for me. I am so thankful that He experienced all the "humanness" of life so that I could find a way to relate to Him on a personal, intimate level. He knows what it feels like to be lonely, tired and hungry. He knows what it feels like to be homesick and to long for the comforts of the familiar. He knows what it feels like to lose a friend. He was betrayed, beaten, mocked, scorned, falsely accused and forsaken. He knows what it feels like to face death. He understands our pain.

And although our salvation was secured through His death and resurrection, I believe that our pathway to fellowship began in His wilderness moments. For, at the very outset of His ministry, He survived a challenge that many of us would have failed. From the beginning of His ministry, He lived by the example that all of us should follow. Even in moments of physical weakness, He walked with God. Even when it must have felt like His days in the wilderness would never end, He walked with God. Even when food was scarce, the enemy was present and loneliness surrounded Him, He walked with God.

Jesus never took His eyes off of the Father. He faced down the tempter with Words of Scripture, and in doing so, He was able to overcome temptations involving power, popularity and compromise...because He walked with God.

Read Genesis 5:24.

Imagine, if you will, being Enoch. One day you are out walking. You take your first step on earth and your next step in heaven. Wow!

Read Hebrews 11:5-6.

Enoch was one who pleased God. He lived a godly life, and it was pleasing to the Father. The Bible tells us that without faith it is impossible to please God (Hebrews 11:6). How is your faith walk? Are you pleasing God? Are you making choices that reflect His love, kindness and purity? Do you put other's interests before your own, or are you too concerned about yourself that you have forgotten how to live a self-less life? Is your heart full of bitterness and hatred; have you refused to offer forgiveness to someone? Are you holding onto the past, or are you able to forget what is behind so that you can look forward to the things God wants for your life?

How are you walking? If your next step takes you into heaven, what type of path will be left behind? A path of kindness and generosity? A path of righteousness? A path of anger and regrets?

Jesus walked down a path to His death so that you and I might live with Him in heaven. He was so tired that He couldn't even carry the weight of the cross on which He was to be crucified. He walked that road for you and for me. What steps are you willing to take for Him?

DAY 14: MY MOMENT IN THE WILDERNESS

Write a prayer thanking Jesus for walking down the road to His crucifixion. Thank Him for dying on the cross for you, or write some thoughts about today's Day in the Desert.

DAY 15: MY PRESENCE GOES WITH YOU

GOD SPEAKS

Jesus,

My Presence will go with You, and I will give You rest.

God

DAY 15: A DAY IN THE DESERT

Read Exodus 33:12-23.

I don't know about you, but I would venture to say that Moses had no idea the magnitude of his request when he said to God, *"Now show me your glory"* (Exodus 33:18). I mean, did Moses really consider that God would actually show up in such a real and powerful way? Can you just imagine what it must have been like to hide in the cleft of a rock while all of God's goodness—His character and His full nature—passed by? Did Moses tremble? Did he cry? Did he hold his breath? Did he fall to the ground? I just wonder.

It is evident from the passage in Exodus 33 that Moses understood, at least to some degree, that God's presence held power. For when he said, *"If your Presence does not go with us, do not send us up from here,"* Moses knew that any journey would be a useless one without the presence of God.

Such is true for our lives as well. The journey is useless unless we are experiencing God's presence—a presence that distinguishes us from all others; a presence that shows we have the favor and pleasure of God.

Read Matthew 17:1-8.

I find it so very interesting that the disciples were not terrified at the sight of Christ's transfiguration. In fact, Peter had enough courage to speak to the transfigured Jesus. Yet, when the bright cloud and the voice of God sounded, they fell facedown to the ground! God's full presence was too powerful to behold. In that beautiful moment of His presence, God was announcing His pleasure in Jesus Christ. Once again, God spoke the words, *"This is my Son, who I love; with him I am well please. Listen to him"* (Matthew 17:5). Peter, James and John probably did not have too much difficulty listening to the words of Christ at that moment. In fact, we know that Peter's experience with God's presence was a powerful one because he writes about it later.

Read 2 Peter 1:16-18.

God's presence was with Jesus as He walked throughout the desert. Is it possible that there could have been a few brief moments when God's glory surrounded Jesus in a bright cloud? Did he hear the voice of His Father saying, *"My Presence will go with you, and I will give you rest"*?

Never have I been wrapped in a visible cloud of God's glory; never have I heard the audible voice of God. But, I know that God's presence has covered me like His hand covered Moses, and I know that God's presence has spoken to me like He spoke to the disciples that day on the sacred mountain. His presence is with me, and like Moses, I don't want to go anywhere without God.

DAY 15: MY MOMENT IN THE WILDERNESS

Are you experiencing God's presence in your life? Does His presence bring rest to your soul? Or, are you striving through the daily demands of life? Write a prayer asking God to give you rest, or write some thoughts about today's Day in the Desert.

DAY 16: GOD OF THE WIND

SCRIPTURE

*But God remembered Noah and all the wild animals
and the livestock that were with him in the ark, and he sent
a wind over the earth, and the waters receded.*

*Then God said to Noah, "Come out of the ark, you
and your wife and your sons and their wives. Bring out
every kind of living creature that is with you—the birds,
the animals, and all the creatures that move along the
ground—so they can multiply on the earth and be fruitful
and increase in number upon it.*

Genesis 8:1, 15-19

JESUS PRAYS

God of the Wind,

A wave of heat rushes over Me in the middle of this day. My
desert surroundings host sizzling temperatures as the wind
makes its way across the wilderness. I sit still, leaning against a tree,
finding shade beneath its branches. The dust is stirring around Me,
yet I am calm and comforted by Your presence.

As I close My eyes, I am reminded of another day, some time
ago, when You moved with power and might. The thought both

saddens Me and amazes Me simultaneously. For I know those You shut inside the ark were safe, dry and well; yet, those upon the earth found their peril. How devastating to know that man's motives had grown to such a wicked level; his heart inclined to constant evil. I still remember the grief of heaven, the pain in My heart as we watched the waters pour from the sky. Men, animals, creatures of both land and sea struck with a sense of fear and dread as the earth was buried under a blanket of heavenly tears; leaving the only source of favor bobbing up and down in a wooden ark.

But what joy filled My soul as I thought of Noah and his family tucked away inside the wooden capsule, an ark of love and safety — a symbol of salvation from the chaos and destruction of the flood. Nothing else remained. Yet, You remembered Noah.

Then, I watched in awe as a great wind moved over the earth. Such might. Such power. To control both wind and rain. The display of strength left heaven silent. For it was as if the angels ceased to breathe as they witnessed the waters receding.

I feel Your wind today. Although a flood of evil tries to engulf Me, I am hidden inside the capsule of Your love and safety. I will not be drowned. For, I know I am protected by Your presence.

I open My eyes. In the distance stands a spotted leopard; he has crept upon his prey unseen and unheard. I remain still, watching. Something stirs, and he darts away with tremendous speed; not unlike the leopard long ago who made his way from the ark. It was a parade of wonder as the door was opened, and animals moved onto dry land. Some scurried off. Others were shy and tried to search out their surroundings before wandering too far into a new habitat. I was amazed at the wonder of it all.

I, too, am like that great ark. For, I am the shelter from the storm. Men can take refuge in Me, and I will save them. For they, too, are like the wild animals in need of shelter. But when the door is opened, when the world beckons to man, what will he do? Some will scurry off to unknown places. Others will show signs of timidity; some never traveling too far from safety. For man has been given so much; allowed to wander and find his way in the open, wild life set before him. Yet, he will never be too far from Your reach. For who can out run the power of the wind? Who can scurry away from Your presence?

A wave of heat rushes over Me. The dust is stirring around Me, and as the wind blows, I know You remember Me.

Jesus

DAY 16: A DAY IN THE DESERT

My husband and I have the most precious cat. He is an orange tabby cat, and we named him Bogey. We both enjoy the game of golf, and I am most familiar with a "bogey." In fact, a triple bogey is not an uncommon score for me. Thus, the inspiration for my cat's name! Bogey is an indoor/outdoor cat. He is free to roam during the day, but we keep him in our garage at night. Every morning, we raise the garage door to let Bogey out for the day. Some mornings he darts under the door with great speed, not even pausing to say, "hello." However, some mornings he is a little more cautious before scurrying into the outside world. It is quite interesting to watch. On those mornings when he hesitates to step out, I often wonder what mischief he has gotten himself into the previous day; for there has to be a reason why he is so timid at times.

Truly, I love my cat. He brings me joy. One of my most favorite things is to watch him when he is "on the hunt." I laugh as he hunkers down, waiting for just the right moment to pounce on an unsuspecting insect. He tickles me as he prowls around the backyard. He looks so serious. In fact, I think he has convinced himself that he is the king of the jungle.

I enjoy the fact that God can use simple things in my life to teach me powerful lessons. All of us are a lot like Bogey. When it comes to venturing out into the unknown, some of us are hesitant. Others scurry on to the next thing in life without taking time to think, pray and process. Some of us love the adventuresome moments of life. And, quite frankly, all of us, at one time or another, have made the mistake of believing that we wear the title "King of the Jungle." Unfortunately, there have been times when all of us have found a comfortable seat on the throne of our lives, rather than submitting to the authority of the King of kings, Jesus Christ.

And, that is the wonder of it all. Even though we go astray at times, even though we make mistakes, and even though we find ourselves in the midst of mischief, God's love still remains.

The Jesus Diaries

Read Genesis 6:5-8.

Doesn't your heart break to know that the Lord was grieved that he had made man? Oh, how sad. I have no way of knowing exactly how God felt at that moment. For there have been things that I have created that I did not like—such as a painting, a cake, a new recipe. Although I was disappointed that my creation did not turn out quite like I had hoped, it did not really grieve me to throw away my work and start again. However, the Bible tells us in Genesis 1:31, *"God saw all that he had made, and it was very good."* God was pleased with what He made; He loved His creation. And, when man's wickedness grew to such a great level of evil, it grieved the heart of God. In fact, the Bible says that *"his heart was filled with pain"* (Genesis 6:6).

And, yet, Noah, a righteous man, found favor with God, and he and his family were saved from God's wrath. Noah was instructed by God to build an ark, and *"Noah and his sons and his wife and his sons' wives entered the ark to escape the waters of the flood. Pairs of clean and unclean animals, of birds and of all creatures that move along the ground, male and female, came to Noah and entered the ark, as God had commanded Noah"* (Genesis 7:7-9).

But every other living thing on the earth was wiped out; *"men and animals and the creatures that move along the ground and the birds of the air were wiped from the earth. Only Noah was left, and those with him in the ark"* (Genesis 7:23). You see, God shut Noah into the ark of safety. Similarly, my husband and I shut Bogey into the garage each night for his safety.

As Christians, we are "shut in" the ark of salvation—Jesus Christ. He is our refuge from the storms, the rains, the floods in our lives, and He provides safety for us. Our circumstances will not always be free of pain and sorrow, but because we are safe inside the Savior's love, we can rest in the assurance that He remembers us just like He remembered Noah. And, when the rain starts falling, when the waters rise, we can trust that our God will tuck us away inside a wooden capsule—an ark of love and safety—salvation from the chaos and destruction of a life without the Son. And, one sweet day, God will send a great wind over the earth, and the "waters" of this life will recede—and we will step into a new surrounding, an eternal home where we will be free to wander and roam. I don't know about you, but when God opens the door and lets me move from this life into the next, I want to scurry into the habitat of heaven without hesitation.

DAY 16: MY MOMENT IN THE WILDERNESS

Are you tucked away inside God's love and protection? Write a prayer of praise to God because of His saving grace, or write some thoughts about today's Day in the Desert.

DAY 17: I WILL BE WITH YOU

GOD SPEAKS

My Son,

When You pass through the waters, I will be with You, and when you pass through the rivers, they will not sweep over You. When You walk through the fire, You will not be burned, the flames will not set You ablaze.

God

DAY 17: A DAY IN THE DESERT

Do you ever just stop and wonder what Jesus and God talked about? I sometimes I wish I could have been "a fly on the wall" when Jesus spent time in prayer. Wouldn't it be fascinating to actually hear a conversation between the Father and the Son? I wonder what they talked about during those desert days? I wonder if they reminisced about creation or if they talked about the schemes of the enemy? To be privy to one sweet exchange between Father and Son would be so amazing. And yet, to some degree, we have been given a glimpse of heavenly conversation. The New Testament records many moments when Jesus assures His audiences that the truth He spoke came from the Father. For example, when Jesus confronted the unbelieving Jews He said, *"For I did not speak of my own accord, but the Father who sent me commanded me what to say and how to say it. I know that his command leads to eternal life. So whatever I say is just what the Father has told me to say"* (John 12:49-50).

I wish I could make that same powerful statement! I wish I could say that all of my conversations have been seasoned with *"what the Father has told me to say."* But, many times I have found myself speaking of my own accord; saying things before I pray, think or ponder on an appropriate response. Can you relate?

Read Daniel 3.

Shadrach, Meshach and Abednego had a powerful response to King Nebuchadnezzar's decree to bow down and worship a golden idol:

*O, Nebuchadnezzar, we do not need to defend ourselves before you in this matter. If we are thrown into the blazing furnace, the God we serve is able to save us from it, and he will rescue us from your hand, O king. But even if he does not, we want you to know, O king, that we will not serve your gods or worship the image of gold you have set up (**Daniel 3:16-17**).*

From the passage in Daniel 3, you read that Shadrach, Meshach and Abednego were thrown into the blazing furnace; however, four men walked around in the fire unharmed. One of the most fascinating parts of this particular story is that when the men emerged from the fiery furnace, *"there was no smell of fire on them"* (Daniel 3:27). Now, if you have ever stood in front of a blazing fire and roasted marshmallows, when you walked away from the fire you were definitely cloaked in a smell of smoke! What a powerful and mighty God we serve!

Read Isaiah 43:2.

Shadrach, Meshach and Abednego walked around in the fire, and they were not set ablaze! Maybe, just maybe God and Jesus reminisced about this event when Jesus was in the desert. They may have talked about the look on O King Nebuchadnezzar's face when he saw not only three men walking around in a blazing furnace unharmed, but four! God could have reminded Jesus that no matter what He would face during His desert days that God's presence would be with Him. He could have reiterated the words of the prophet Isaiah. I just wonder. Like I said, listening in on one of their conversations would be pretty powerful.

And, yet, I still rejoice because we have been given the Bible—which is a real, genuine conversation that we can have with the Father. As we read the pages of Scripture, we can hear the voice of the One who loves us, we can recognize the truth found in the written Word, and we can rest assured that even if He didn't speak the words of Isaiah 43:2 to Jesus in the desert, He still spoke. And, He still speaks today.

DAY 17: MY MOMENT IN THE WILDERNESS

What is God saying to you today? Write some thoughts about today's Day in the Desert.

DAY 18: GOD OF THE LONELY

SCRIPTURE

The angel of the Lord found Hagar near a spring in the desert; it was the spring that is beside the road to Shur. And he said, "Hagar, servant of Sarai, where have you come from, and where are you going?"

"I'm running away from my mistress Sarai," she answered.

Then the angel of the Lord told her, "Go back to your mistress and submit to her." The angel added, "I will so increase your descendents that they will be too numerous to count."

She gave this name to the Lord who spoke to her: "You are the God who sees me," for she said, "I have now seen the One who sees me."

Genesis 16:7-10, 13

JESUS PRAYS

God of the Lonely,

Were it not for the presence of You, My heart would break from loneliness. Even as I find solace in You I still long for the fellowship of family and friends. For We are complete and One, and Our love is pure without bounds. Yet, to be loved by the ones We created is to know a joy without end.

Here I am without human companionship; physically alone on My solitary journey with the tempter. Knowing full well You sit with Me and visit Me here gives life to My soul. Yet, humanly, I am still alone.

I remember another who sat alone in the desert plagued with a need to know true and lasting love. Even now I cannot shake the look of desperation on her face as she sat beside the stream. For, she was on the road to Shur, yet completely unaware of her destination. She was pregnant; not of her will but because of her place in life. A servant mistreated by her lady, heartbroken, angry and afraid. She was in the throws of despair; a runaway with no one to care for her; nowhere to turn; longing for a complete, pure, boundless love.

But Your eye, the one that sees the sparrow, saw her that day. You knew her coming and her going. She was not alone. For just as she claimed, You are El Roi; You are the God who sees. Just as You see Me now; alone in this desert place.

I am here, and here I will stay. For I shall not deter from My purpose. To walk away from this calling is to turn My back upon all those who will sit in the desert alone. How can I leave the ones I love in their moment of need? How can I break this bond of compassion? Loneliness may be My nearest companion at this moment, and I may long for a way out of this wilderness; yet, I shall remain. My body may ache for food, My heart may ache for the company of others, but My soul shall rejoice. For in You My joy is complete. As the psalmist proclaimed:

You know when I sit and when I rise; you perceive my thoughts from afar. You discern my going out and my lying down; you are familiar with all my ways. Before a word is on my tongue you know it completely. You hem me in—behind and before; you have laid your hand upon me. Where can I go from your Spirit? Where can I flee from your presence? If I go up to the heavens, you are there; if I make my bed in the depths, you are there. If I rise on the wings of the dawn, if I settle on the far side of the sea, even there your hand will guide me, your right hand will hold me fast (Psalm 139:2-5, 7-10).

For You are the God who sees Me. In My wilderness moment, I am not alone. And the ones I love shall never face the wilderness without Me. Because I have been here, My Spirit can attest to their pain; My heart understands. As I once visited with Hagar in her desert moment, I shall then visit each lonely soul—and I will empower him with the strength to overcome and return home—home to a place of safety and protection; home to those who will love and comfort; home to the One who will satisfy his soul. For I will endure this desert moment for the joy of moments to come; moments when My love will be returned by the ones who come back home.

Jesus

DAY 18: A DAY IN THE DESERT

I do not know the emotional pain Jesus may have experienced while He was in the desert. I am not sure if He felt loneliness, but I do know that you and I are the reason for whatever suffering He may have encountered. Does it overwhelm you to consider that truth? Jesus did not have to endure any kind of heartache for us, but He did. At any point during His earthly life He could have forsaken us and returned to His home in glory, but He endured. He finished the work of salvation because He loves us with an enormous love!

Can you ever remember a time when you felt totally alone? Have you been abandoned by a spouse, a mother, a father or a friend? Have any of your children forsaken their godly upbringing and travelled down a path of unrighteousness? Have you experienced moments of isolation? Do you remember the agony? Have you ever felt completely forgotten? Maybe you feel that way this very moment.

I remember feeling forgotten. For whatever reason, God did not allow me to marry until I was almost 37 years old. I watched my friends and family members marry and have two and three children before I had the privilege of walking down the aisle. There were moments that I truly struggled with feeling like God had forgotten all about me. It seemed like everyone else around me received blessings from God, and I felt alone. Although I walked with God during those moments of singleness (and there were tremendous blessings in my life during those days), I still wondered at times if He overlooked me by accident when He was handing out the blessing of marriage.

The truth is God had not at all forgotten me. And, I would venture to say that in those wilderness moments of my life when I cried out to Him, when tears were streaming down my face, that God's heart was full of compassion and love for me. All along, God had a plan for me. All along, He knew I would marry. His timing was simply different from mine.

And, now, looking back on my life and those moments of pain during my singleness—I would not change anything. God strengthened my heart and my life through some of those lonely moments.

He taught me how to depend on Him for my every need, and He showed me that a husband is a tremendous treasure yet God is the greatest blessing of all. And, even in the darkest days of my life when I longed for human companionship, I cried out to the Lover of my soul, and He saw me, comforted me and gave me the love I so desperately needed.

Read Matthew 27:45-46.

Jesus was hanging on a cross when He cried the words found in Matthew 27:46. He experienced total abandonment when He took on the sins of the world and became the sacrificial Lamb for all of us. Friend, Jesus may not have suffered loneliness in His desert days, but He felt forsaken when He bore the weight of our sin on the cross. The utter loneliness that He experienced only makes Him that much more personal and approachable.

Because Jesus endured the cross alone, we can trust and believe that He understands our pain. When all of our friends are celebrating weddings and we are still single, Jesus understands. When we have prayed for a baby and the pregnancy test is negative, Jesus understands. When our spouses abandon us for another life and we are left alone, Jesus understands. When we are the last ones standing on the playground and everyone else has been picked for a team, Jesus understands. He knows the emotional agony of feeling forgotten and forsaken. Jesus knows. And, yet, in those moments when it seems like we are completely invisible to the rest of the world, God knows where to find us. Just like God saw Hagar in her distress, He sees you too. You do not suffer alone.

Read Genesis 16.

Allow me to ask you a few questions: Are you running away from your life? Are you, like Hagar, sitting in a desert of loneliness and heartbrokenness? Do you feel like crying out, "My God, my God, why have you forsaken me?" If so, then please take heart. God sees you. He has not forgotten you. You are not forsaken.

In Deuteronomy 31:8, Moses said these words to Joshua: *"The Lord himself goes before you and will be with you; he will never leave you nor forsake you. Do not be afraid; do not be discouraged."*

May the words Moses spoke so long ago be a comfort to you during your lonely moments.

DAY 18: MY MOMENT IN THE WILDERNESS

Are you discouraged today? Are you lonely? Write a prayer asking God for comfort and peace, or write some thoughts about today's Day in the Desert.

DAY 19: I AM FAITHFUL

GOD SPEAKS

Jesus,

I am faithful, and I will strengthen and protect you from the evil one.

God

DAY 19: A DAY IN THE DESERT

As we read the passages of Scripture, we are taught that God is loyal, dependable and faithful. He fulfills all of His promises; that fact is hard for some of us to believe because we make the mistake of placing our hope and trust in fallible human beings. Unfortunately, when we are disappointed, cheated and deceived, our hearts become afraid to trust. Sometimes after we have been hurt, we become guarded in the area of relationships.

Maybe you have faced some trying circumstances in your life, and you feel disappointed in God. Questions may loom in your mind about God's goodness because your husband now lies in the arms of another, your son's body now lies in a grave or your dream home now lies in a pile of ash. You may feel cheated, deceived or disillusioned. And, quite frankly, you may blame it all on God.

There are moments when our emotions deceive us; moments when we have difficulty trusting God and believing that what He says is true. Yet, even in those times when we choose to ignore God, when we are giving Him the "silent treatment" because we do not agree with Him or because we do not understand the purpose in our suffering, He is still a loving and good God. Our momentary afflictions and feelings cannot change the fact that God is good.

Read Psalm 62:11-2 and Psalm 59:9, 17.

As I write this today, I am overwhelmed by the events in our lives that seem unfair such as children dying in car accidents, countries wracked by diseases, infants born addicted to drugs, employees losing jobs, promotions based on politics rather than merit, dishonest business practices leading to millions while the honest man works for minimum wage, the drunk driver who walks away from the wreckage while the teenaged driver is loaded into an ambulance. Life is unfair at times.

But, as I write this today, I am even more overwhelmed by the events in the wilderness. Is it fair that Jesus suffered for you and me? Is it fair that His lips may have cracked and His skin dried out from exposure to the sun? Is it fair that He was hungry and tired and tested and tried? What did Jesus ever do to deserve suffering? How do we justify His pain? How can we ignore the fact that He was offered everything that we long for in this world—popularity, fame, wealth and power—and yet, He chose death on a cross so that we could have eternal life? He gave up everything for us—His home in heaven, His life—so that we would not have to die a spiritual death and live in separation from a loving God! Jesus was humiliated, nailed to a cross and forsaken, so that we could be exalted, set free from sin and remembered forever! None of that is fair.

In those moments when we want to blame God for our circumstances, we need to turn to the truth of His word.

Read Psalm 145:9, 13-20.

I openly confess that I do not understand the unfair things in this life; however, I do agree with Paul when he said:

> *I consider that our present sufferings are not worth comparing with the glory that will be revealed in us. And we know that in all things God works for the good of those who love him, who have been called according to his purpose. No, in all these things we are more than conquerors through him who loved us* (Romans 8:18, 28, 37).

When you find yourself having a hard time believing and trusting in God, try to remember the words of Numbers 24:19, "*God is not a man, that he should lie, nor a son of man, that he should change his mind. Does he speak and then not act? Does he promise and not fulfill?*"

Placing your hope in human beings and in your circumstances will always bring disappointment, but when you put your hope in God, He will bring peace to your days of wilderness suffering. Allow Him to heal the broken and wounded places in your heart. Look to Him, because at the proper time He will open His hand to satisfy you.

DAY 19: MY MOMENT IN THE WILDERNESS

Are you holding a grudge against God today? Are you afraid to trust Him because things in your life have not gone according to your plan? Talk to Him about it today. Write a prayer or some thoughts about today's Day in the Desert.

DAY 20: GOD OF MIRTH

SCRIPTURE

Is anything too hard for the Lord? I will return to you at the appointed time next year and Sarah will have a son.

Genesis 18:14

JESUS PRAYS

God of Mirth,

His laughter breaks out across the barrenness, and although I am in a sweltering and arid land, the sound of it chills My soul. He is the epitome of evil, and at this moment I am grateful for My lack of food; for My stomach churns at his mere presence. The sound of his cackle is foreboding.

But he shall not laugh last. For the triumphant sound of Your glee shall ring into eternity. I shall serve as his object of amusement but only for a moment, and I am none too glad.

Laughter is a funny thing; it accompanies us in various moments — moments of surprise, moments of bewilderment, moments of joy. Some laugh when anxious, others when afraid. Laughter is melodious when with someone; malicious when towards someone; having the power to both heal and pierce the soul. Laughter is found living within the young and old alike; displaying itself in the midst of children as they draw in the sand, and weaving itself throughout conversations at a family affair.

Laughter joins and separates; unites and divides—it can align one side against another or bring all to a consensus. Laughter has power—it stirs the souls, ignites the soul, stills the soul. Laughter is real.

I remember the day she laughed. I know You do too. For her husband laughed when he learned she would be the mother of nations. *"Abraham fell face down; he laughed and said to himself, 'Will a son be born to a man a hundred years old? Will Sarah bear a child at the age of ninety?'"* (Genesis 17:17) Abraham, although a friend, laughed at what seemed preposterous.

And Sarah too. For how ludicrous it must have sounded to her barren hope to hear that she would bring forth a child. Disbelief. Scorning the impossible. She, and the company around her, knew far too well that her body was beyond its years of motherhood. Is not that the beautiful irony of it all? Will man never comprehend that nothing can confine God; that no human constraint can deter Your power? As was once spoken to Sarah, *"Is anything too hard for the Lord?"* (Genesis 18:14).

If she had only known the whole story. If she had only believed in the impossible. At the moment the promise was spoken she would have celebrated with shouts of jubilation. Her laughter would have awakened the dormant hope inside; she would have chuckled without shame—giggled with the wonder of it all. If she had only known she would be a mother to the bloodline that would deliver Me. If she had only known.

And if he, My enemy, only knew, he would laugh no more. For now he celebrates in ignorance, yet someday he will grieve in full knowledge. The pleasure of his pride now shows itself in the sound of his snicker—and I know I will hear such laughter in the coming days. When sin is placed upon My back and the melody of heaven is silenced; it is his cacophony I will hear—the sound of dissonance and discord as You turn from Me.

Although I know his glory is short-lived, I still shudder at his jollity. I am the subject of his scorn; for he laughs at, not with Me.

But, that is the beautiful paradox of it all. He laughs, yet he laughs in vain.

For when he thinks the battle has ended, it is Your voice I will hear; it is Your laughter I will dance to when You shout, "Arise! Come forth!" And then, with You, I shall laugh out loud—as angels in victory sing. And with that thought, I cannot help but smile—even now, while he laughs at Me.

Jesus

DAY 20: A DAY IN THE DESERT

Read Genesis 18:1-15.

Have you ever found yourself in Sarah's position—laughing, or rather scoffing, at something which seemed absolutely impossible? I have. I am amazed when I see old, worn out cars on the expressway. I am amazed that these vehicles, sputtering black smoke, can even make it out of the driveway. What amazes me even more is when these same vehicles have luggage tied to the roof, five people packed inside the car, and it is moving down the interstate! I catch myself laughing, wondering if the car will actually carry its passengers to their final destination because to me, it doesn't look likely.

I remember the day my friend and I drove our cars along Cobb Parkway in Marietta, Georgia, utterly amazed that the next day we would actually run in a 6.2 mile race on that exact road. The course looked like an uphill climb much more difficult than we imagined while training. I will never forget, upon seeing the actual course, how we both laughed out loud, wondering if we had taken on an impossible feat!

We scoff at trivial things in life; however, sometimes we laugh at the meaningful things in life. We laugh when someone tells us, "Let go and let God." We laugh when we hear people say, "There really is light at the end of the tunnel." We laugh when we hear someone say, "God answers prayer."

We say to our friends, "What? My husband, take out the trash? Are you kidding?" And we laugh. We say to our coworkers, "My wife, cook? You must have her confused with someone else." And, we laugh. We say to our parents, "Why did I get married?" And we laugh. We say to the divorce attorney, "Thanks for the favor." And, we laugh.

Not the grandpa-told-a-knee-slapper kind of laugh. It's more like a sneer, as if we are making fun of the life that we have—as if we are ridiculing our circumstances and the people in our lives. We laugh with unbelief—we laugh with sarcasm, believing full well in our hearts that blessings are impossible.

Sarah laughed, but she was not laughing with joy. She, at the time, believed motherhood was impossible for her. And, when she heard the Lord proclaim that she would have a son, she laughed in unbelief.

Want to hear something funny?

Now the Lord was gracious to Sarah as he had said, and the Lord did for Sarah what he had promised. Sarah became pregnant and bore a son to Abraham in his old age, at the very time God had promised him. Abraham gave the name Isaac to the son Sarah bore him (Genesis 21:1-3).

The name Isaac means "he laughs."

"Sarah said, 'God has brought me laughter, and everyone who hears about this will laugh with me.' And she added, 'Who would have said to Abraham that Sarah would nurse children? Yet I have borne him a son in his old age'" (Genesis 21:6-7).

I believe at this point in her life, Sarah's laugh was filled with wonder, awe and amazement at God and His blessing in her life. What she once scorned, she now embraced with joy.

What are the things in your life that cause you to laugh in unbelief? Are you struggling with a power-hungry boss? Have you given up on your spouse? Are you tired of trying to communicate with your teenager? Did you stop praying for a particular person because it seemed useless? Do you scoff at the balance in your bank account?

I agree that there are moments in life when our circumstances do not cause great joy. There are moments when things look impossible; when blessings seem like they are falling on everyone else around us and we are left standing with nothing. And, in those moments it is much easier to laugh with a heart filled with sarcasm than with a heart filled with hope.

Never would I try to make light of another's circumstances. I know that life has its moments of deep pain; I have experienced some of those moments. We all have. But I still believe that we can trust God. I still believe He answers prayer. I still believe that we can laugh a wholesome laugh because the Lord is the joy of our salvation.

And, I truly believe that our Lord will have the last laugh! Satan may have taunted Jesus in the wilderness. He may have laughed when Jesus gave up His life on the cross. He may laugh now when Christians make mistakes and fall out of fellowship with God. But, these will be the only days he laughs. I believe that there is a day when Jesus will set everything right, and Satan's reign will end.

You might not be at a place in your life today where you can laugh with joy, so for you I echo the words of Paul, *"May the God of hope fill you with all joy and peace as you trust in him, so that you may overflow with hope by the power of the Holy Spirit"* (Romans 15:13).

DAY 20: MY MOMENT IN THE WILDERNESS

Evaluate your life today. In what areas do you find yourself laughing? Is your heart filled with joyful laughter, or do you scoff at your circumstances? Write a prayer or some thoughts about today's Day in the Desert.

DAY 21: GOD OF THE RIGHTEOUS

_꒰ꑄ꒱_

SCRIPTURE

Shall I hide from Abraham what I am about to do? Abraham will surely become a great nation, and all nations on earth will be blessed through him. For I have chosen him so that he will direct his children and his household after him to keep the way of the Lord by doing what is right and just, so that the Lord will bring about for Abraham what he has promised him.

The men turned away and went toward Sodom, but Abraham remained standing before the Lord.

Genesis 18:17-19, 22

JESUS PRAYS

God of the Righteous,

The days in the desert are trying. Moments spent here weaken My body, yet My Spirit soars. I know I shall not dwell here eternally; for My lot in this wilderness is temporal. If I should give into the adversary, Our purpose is thwarted. So, I shall remain standing, just as Abraham stood, and because I do not sit at the enemy's feet, the promise remains. I will not walk away. I bear this hardship for man; I challenge the enemy now so that mankind will confront him in coming days. Though I do not enjoy this momentary affliction, I endure out of love for man. I want him to be with Me. I want to save him. And I know that My suffering is by Your hand; therefore, it is right.

I remember when Abraham spoke the words:

Will you sweep away the righteous with the wicked? Far be if from you to do such a thing—to kill the righteous with the wicked, treating the righteous and the wicked alike. Far be it from you! Will not the Judge of all the earth do right? (Genesis 18:23, 25)

He stood before his tent; the look in his eyes intense as a sense of urgency consumed him. His compassion for his relatives mirrors My merciful heart towards the ones You love. For like Abraham, I, too, believe that there are righteous men among the wicked. For like Abraham, I, too, stand before you and implore. For just as he pled for the city of Sodom, I shall plead for his descendants; those who have turned from truth; those who know You not. For, even before there was a beginning, I pledged to intercede for man. I shall not renege; I shall not make void My word.

Although My muscles ache within Me, I shall not find this My last day in the wilderness. And even when My weary feet refuse to walk this desert terrain, I shall remain. For I am the promise; I am the guarantee. Should My presence in this place cease, mankind would die—the enemy would win. Even now he meets with Me, longing for My allegiance, trying with all of his effort to break Me. He tries to destroy what You promised long ago to Abraham; he tries to extinguish the covenant between You and the father of all nations.

For I know Your plan; I was there when it was set in motion, and because of that I shall not give into the schemes of the covenant breaker. I shall not allow the enemy to nullify the treaty between You and Your friend Abraham. For I shall be the instrument You use to bring the promise to fruition. My heart is bound by the covenant promise; My love is backed by the assurance of the word You spoke long ago. My life will be the fulfillment of Abraham's long awaited hope. And, as I make supplication before You for those sons and daughters as numerous as the stars, I know, as Abraham did, that You will do right. You will bring about Your purpose. You will destroy the wicked; yet the righteous shall remain.

Jesus

DAY 21: A DAY IN THE DESERT

Read Genesis 18:16-33.

Are you ever completely astonished by the things that you read in Scripture? The Lord actually tells Abraham about His plan to judge the city of Sodom and Gomorrah. Not only does He speak to Abraham about His plan, He allows Abraham to have a voice before the Lord! Abraham pleads with God, the Judge, for the lives of the righteous living among the wicked in Sodom and Gomorrah. And, here is the best part—God listens! When Abraham asks for God to spare 50, 45, 40, 30, 20, 10 people from His wrath, God pays attention. And, each time Abraham approaches God with another request, God is patient, loving and kind.

In Genesis 18:32, we hear the Lord speak these words, *"For the sake of ten, I will not destroy it."* But, Genesis 19 informs us that Sodom and Gomorrah were destroyed, which leads us to believe that God was unable to find even 10 righteous people in the city. I find it interesting, however, that God remembered Abraham.

"So when God destroyed the cities of the plain, he remembered Abraham, and he brought Lot out of the catastrophe that overthrew the cities where Lot had lived" **(Genesis 19:29).**

Lot was Abraham's nephew.

Do you plead with God for the ones you love? Do you speak to Him on behalf of the righteous? Evaluate your prayer life. When you stand before God, what do you say to Him? What are you asking of the Lord?

Abraham knew that God was righteous. He knew that God would make the right decision about Sodom and Gomorrah. And, I think that knowledge gave Abraham the courage to approach the throne of justice in order to ask God to spare the city for 10 righteous people. He took a stand because he knew he could depend upon the "rightness" of God.

We could all take a lesson from Abraham. As we get to know the Father more, we begin to grasp the many facets of His character. We can approach Him with the courage to ask for provision when we trust that He is the One who provides. We can approach Him with the strength to ask for healing when we trust that He is the One who heals. As we see Him merciful, we find courage to ask for mercy. As we see Him loving, we find strength to ask for love.

When we recognize the character of God, we begin to trust the heart of God. We begin to believe that God is fair, honest and even-handed. And that belief gives us the courage to take a stand before the Father.

I wonder how many times someone has taken a "stand" for me. Truly, I wonder how many righteous men and women have taken time to pray for me; to plead for me; to approach the throne of heaven and ask God to take care of me.

I wonder, too, if Jesus took a stand for me while He was in the wilderness. Did He lie awake at night, staring at the stars in the sky, remembering God's promise to Abraham in Genesis 15:5? Did He count the stars and think of me—one of Abraham's offspring? Did He think about you?

Galatians 3:29 says, *"If you belong to Christ, then you are Abraham's seed, and heirs according to the promise."*

Did Jesus endure the wilderness and overcome Satan's temptation because He was pleading for our lives? God made a covenant with Abraham, and because of Christ's death, burial and resurrection, all Christians are a part of that covenant fulfillment. Jesus could have broken the deal. He could have taken one step in the desert and the next step in glory. He did not have to walk the wilderness road, and He did not have to hang on a tree and die for us. But, He did. Jesus took a stand for us when He gave His life on the cross. And, now, when I look into the heavens and count the stars in the sky, I know that I am an heir to throne because of a promise made so long ago.

DAY 21: MY MOMENT IN THE WILDERNESS

What if Jesus really did lie on the desert floor, look up at the stars in the sky and think about you. Do you ever consider that you are on His mind; that He thinks of you? Write a prayer or some thoughts about today's Day in the Desert.

DAY 22: GOD OF GREAT SACRIFICE

~ꞬꞋꞬ~

SCRIPTURE

Abraham took the wood for the burnt offering and placed it on his son Isaac, and he himself carried the fire and the knife.

Genesis 22:6

JESUS PRAYS

God of Great Sacrifice,

This morning, as I walk through this dusty terrain, a rock catches My eye. With no specific thought or reason, I walk in its direction. Instinctively, I pile several stones together. I am reminded of Abraham. For, he built many altars upon places of spiritual experience. I must say that this experience for Me is quite memorable, and as I build My makeshift structure, I am drawn into Your beautiful presence. For You alone are the object of My worship and praise, and for You I will be sacrificed and spilt. I am fully aware that even as I face the tempter that I am not alone; for, You meet with Me here. You provide Me with the strength to remember that Your plan will triumph.

As in days of old, You met with Abraham; You appeared to him to remind him that his offspring would inherit the land of the Canaanites. In that place, where he met with You, he built an altar before You. And, once again, in Bethel—where he pitched his tent— he made for You a gathering of stones and called upon Your name.

Today, it I who calls upon Your name, and as I sit among these rocks, as I recognize the Sacrifice, I call to You. For, without Your provision through these days of wilderness calling, I shall not make it to rest upon the table of surrender which awaits Me. Thus, I beseech You to visit with Me in this place and enable Me to lay siege upon the enemy who longs to assassinate Me. He longs to bind My being to the adoration of his name; he salivates at the idea that I may bow to the throne of power he lingers before Me. He desires to know that these stones around Me are placed in his honor. But, My praise he will never receive. My admiration he will never obtain. For this heap of stones does not represent My love for the enemy; it represents My disdain for him. It represents his end, his doom, his ultimate peril.

I am bound to this altar as Isaac was bound by his father. Yet unlike Isaac, I will not be released from the pile of wood. I will not be removed from the place of slaughter. A ram will not rescue Me from the moment of offering. For this altar holds the Rock that will bleed over the nations. The righteous blood of this spotless Lamb will be the atoning sacrifice for all mankind.

Jesus

DAY 22: A DAY IN THE DESERT

We read in Genesis 15:1-5 God's promise to Abram (Abraham) that he would have an heir.

> *After this, the word of the Lord came to Abram (**Abraham**) in a vision: "Do not be afraid, Abram. I am your shield, your very great reward."*
>
> *But Abram said, "O sovereign Lord, what can you give me since I remain childless and the one who will inherit my estate is Eliezar of Damascus?" And Abram said, "You have given me no children; so a servant in my household will be my heir."*
>
> *Then the word of the Lord came to him: "This man will not be your heir, but a son coming from your own body will be your heir." He took him outside and said, "Look up at the heavens and count the stars—if indeed you can count them."*
>
> *Then he said to him, "So shall your offspring be." Abram believed the Lord, and he credited it to him as righteousness.*

We know that Abraham and Sarah conceived Isaac in their old age, so it may have seemed like God's promise would never come to fruition; however, God was faithful, and Isaac was born.

Read Genesis 22:1-18.

This Biblical story is so fascinating to me. The faith of Abraham and Sarah seems to be tested in monumental ways! After waiting so long for an heir, now God wants Abraham to take his only son and sacrifice him on an altar! Wow!

The faith of Abraham is simply astounding. I truly do not understand how anyone could have the emotional strength to hike up to the top of a mountain—knowing all along that very walk led to a son's death. Abraham believed that God would fulfill the promise spoken in Genesis 15. So, Abraham must have believed that God would bless him with another heir or raise Isaac from the dead. Either way, Abraham obeyed—even though he was unsure how God would keep His word. And it was his faith in God and his obedience to God that gave Abraham the courage to bind his son and place him on an altar. The Bible says that Abraham took the knife and was ready to slay Isaac when the angel of the Lord called out to him and told him to stop! What submission. I wonder if I could be so faithful if placed in the same situation.

Do you ever wonder what took place between Abraham and Isaac? Did they struggle as Abraham bound Isaac? Or, did Isaac willingly allow his father to place him on an altar of sacrifice? Maybe Isaac believed that Abraham knew what he was doing. Maybe he trusted his father. Maybe he did go to the altar willingly.

While in the Garden of Gethsemane, Jesus prayed and asked God to "remove the cup." If there was any other way for man to enter into fellowship with God, Jesus wanted to take that route. Jesus certainly did not want to suffer and die, but He was obedient to God's plan. He went to the cross willingly for us because He knew there was no other way for us to have the forgiveness of sins. He had to become the sacrifice for all of us in order for us to have access to God.

I have no idea how long Jesus knew that He would suffer on the cross. Maybe He knew from the time He could actually think. Maybe He knew at the age of twelve when He sat in the temple among the teachers asking and answering questions. The gospels teach us that He predicted His death, so He was aware that He would be sacrificed for our sin. Maybe He knew when He was in the wilderness. And, maybe during His wilderness moments He was reminded that the only way we could be saved was if He fulfilled the calling placed on His life—if He indeed died on the cross for the sins of all. Maybe that knowledge, along with His complete and total reliance upon God and His Word, gave Jesus the strength He needed to endure Satan's temptation.

There is one last thing that fascinates me about the story of Abraham and Isaac. Did you catch the fact that it was Isaac who carried the wood on his shoulders as he climbed the mountain? The very altar on which Isaac was to die, he himself carried up the mountain. Does that strike you as amazing? The picture is a beautiful foreshadowing of Jesus, who carried the wood on which He would be sacrificed—the cross on which He would die.

Today, I am grateful that God provided a ram for Abraham, so that Isaac did not have to die. The ram was a substitutionary sacrifice—just as Christ's death was a substitute for my death. Today, I am grateful that God provided the Lamb, so that I could be redeemed!

Read Mark 10:45.

DAY 22: MY MOMENT IN THE WILDERNESS

You have been redeemed! Write a prayer thanking Jesus for His great sacrifice, or write some thoughts about today's Day in the Desert.

DAY 23: GOD OF ALL

SCRIPTURE

"I tell you," he replied, "if they keep quiet, the stones will cry out."

Luke 19:40

JESUS PRAYS

God of All,

I know that Your mighty voice called all things into being, and that You placed things here in this desert home for a purpose and a reason. Yet, some might wonder at Your intention for a simple desert rock. Quite frankly, it really does not look too very different from the rocks which are nestled beside it, and it is not a pretty one at that. On rare occasions a lion perches upon it while he scans the desert for prey. The coney sometimes snuggles its way inside the rock's crevices for safety and rest. Every once in a while the snake finds his comfort in the sun upon a rock's back. But, for the most part the desert rock is dull, with little meaning or purpose.

For it does not rest in the bottom of the ocean as a hiding place for fish. It does not sit in the middle of the prairie surrounded by a mix of beautiful wildflowers. It is not a resting place for the shepherd as he watches his flocks by night. No, it is a simple desert rock soaking in the heat of its surroundings and adding very little color to this terrain. In fact, as one looks across the landscape, this rock does not stand out—no, instead it blends in with all that encamps it.

And yet, I see its beauty—even in such a desolate wasteland? For even now, as I shuffle along with quite a slow pace, I see its purpose. For I am weary; struggling to take My next step. I have a deep need for sleep.

With steps that are ever-so-labored, I near the desert rock, My bed—My pillow for the night. As I approach the rock, I can sense the praise dwelling inside of it. O, that it had a mouth—for I know it would cry out in worship! I know it would proclaim, *"He is the Rock, his works are perfect, and all his ways are just. A faithful God who does no wrong, upright and just is he"* (Deuteronomy 32:4). It would cry out to the heavens, *"May the words of my mouth and the meditation of my heart be pleasing in your sight, O Lord, My Rock and my Redeemer"* (Psalm 19:14).

So now I say to this simple stone, "Oh dear, dull desert rock, the Lord of all—the Rock of Salvation—rests His weary head upon you—for you are a place of comfort—a refuge to Me. As I slumber, you will hold Me. For you are useful. Once something of seemingly little value, yet, now you cradle the King!"

Jesus

DAY 23: A DAY IN THE DESERT

I don't know about you, but there are countless days in my life when I have felt like the rock in that story. Moments filled with questions about my usefulness; my purpose. For, all of us long to be special; each of us wants to know that we have a significant place here on this earth. I would venture to say that all of us would like to know that we have contributed to a greater cause; that we have made this world a better place just by being here day in and day out.

Maybe your life has a little more flash than the life of the dull rock in the desert? Maybe you shine in the classroom or soar in the boardroom. It could be that your physical appearance brings you attention or your skills on the soccer field bring you success. Maybe your education gave you the edge you needed to get that well-paying job, and maybe your antics in the courtroom help you win case after case after case. So, you probably don't look quite as boring as a desert rock. But are you?

Or, maybe you can totally relate to a rock who feels like he just blends in with his surroundings. Maybe you do not sense that you are special or wanted or cared for. It could be that you are just like every other person in your crowd of friends or at your work place. Maybe your husband has stopped looking at you like he used to before the bills and kids and demanding job. Maybe your children have forgotten you because they like the new-found freedom that a driver's license brings. Maybe you feel like a dull, ugly rock in a desert of rocks just like you; nothing special, nothing unique; just plain you.

There were countless rocks in the desert; many places where our Savior could have taken a short nap or slumbered throughout the night. But, in that very moment when He chose one rock—one particular rock to lay His weary head, Christ brought a distinct purpose and meaning to the life of that rock.

Have you had such an encounter with Jesus Christ? Have you found your purpose and your significance in the Lord?

Regardless of our place, status or position in life; regardless of how we may feel at the present moment, all of us (every single one of us) need an encounter with Jesus Christ. Our purpose, our significance, our place is only found in the Lord. And when you allow the Spirit of God to rest and live inside your life, you become a cradle to the King; you become His dwelling place. How much more exciting does life get than that?

All of us have, at one time or another, had questions about Jesus. Who is He? Is Jesus really the Son of God? Can Jesus really take away all of my sins? If I trust in Jesus, will He really do what He promises to do in my life? We have all wondered at this man Jesus, and we have all looked upon Him with curiosity and with a careful eye.

When is the last time you became overwhelmed and excited at the presence of God in your life? Do you remember? Have you ever grown so completely and utterly amazed at the fact that Christ sees you—that He knows you—that in a landscape of rocks just like you that He has chosen you? He has not overlooked you.

You have such significance and worth.

Read Zephaniah 3:17.

Take comfort in knowing that God loves you.

DAY 23: MY MOMENT IN THE WILDERNESS

Do you believe that you are significant to God? Write a prayer of praise to the Lord today, or write some thoughts about today's Day in the Desert.

DAY 24: THE ONE WHO WRESTLES

~⟨∿⟩~

SCRIPTURE

Then the man said, "Your name will no longer be Jacob, but Israel, because you have struggled with God and with men and have overcome."
So Jacob called the place Peniel, saying, "It is because I saw God face to face, and yet my life was spared."
Genesis 32:28, 30

JESUS PRAYS

The One Who Wrestles,

The light of Your face shines down on Your servant today. Oh, how I relish in the radiance of Your presence; how I desire for man to know such glory—not of his own, but God's glory—to bask in the warmth of knowing Jehovah. Yet, man struggles; he wrestles with desires that turn him away; desires that divide his loyalties.

How My heart yearns for all men to see Your splendor—the beauty of Your face—the promised land. Even now, as I consider the Israelites—as I remember their hard hearts and utter rebellion—My heart aches. For even when the way was clear to them, they chose to act of their own accord—chose not to submit to Your ways—a disobedience that led them through the wilderness. Oh how they struggled—how they wrestled and fought with their Deliverer. And as I share with them now in My own moment of wilderness, My heart breaks over their stubbornness. For each day spent here represents one year of their wandering, their searching, their rebellion. But I say to the enemy, "Meet with Me face to face." I challenge him to an all out war—for I am not afraid to wrestle with evil. I shall do whatever it takes to win back the souls of men. For I am determined to lead My people from the wilderness of ruin into Glory.

I look to Your face today—Your face I seek, and I beg You to be gracious to man. Bless him. May Your face shine upon him. Pour Your light into his heart and give him the knowledge of salvation. Oh, what a beautiful day it will be when man stands before You— face to face—and experiences the magnificent wonder and fullness of the Most High!

But, until then, I know he will struggle. I know he will wrestle against all that is good and right. I remember full well how Jacob struggled—how he fought first with Esau in the womb, how he battled his way to a birth right blessing, how he persevered seven more years to receive his bride, and how he wrestled through the night with You. Oh, he was determined; driven to get ahead—refusing to cave into pressure. Jacob never quit. He never gave up!

And, I, too, shall never surrender to the enemy's pleas. I shall not turn from brilliant light to the darkness of death. For, I have seen Your face and the beauty it contains; I have beheld pure love, total perfection, blazing glory—and I shall never look away.

For, I am that face of Glory; I am the revelation of a Holy God. He who has seen Me has seen the Father. For, when man looks upon Me, it is Your face he will see—a face of compassion and mercy—a face of forgiveness and grace.

Jesus

DAY 24: A DAY IN THE DESERT

Read Genesis 32:22-30.

When is the last time you struggled with God? Are you struggling with Him today? Is there something happening in your life that is causing your faith to waver? Are you waiting to hear God speak to you? What are you dealing with in your life today? Is sin keeping you from experiencing all that God has to offer you, or are you, like Job, blameless and upright—yet struggling?

Jacob understood what it meant to fight with God. He understood the importance of holding onto God for answers and insight. The Bible says in Genesis 32:26, *"But Jacob replied, 'I will not let you go unless you bless me.'"*

True blessing comes from God, and Jacob wanted to hold on for a blessing. He was persistent.

As you wrestle with the truths of God, do not let your pride or your own self-sufficiency get in the way of your relationship with God. God is much more powerful than we are, and it is only by His strength in our lives that we are able to endure. God allowed Jacob to wrestle with Him for a moment, yet He did touch the socket of Jacob's hip and weakened him—simply to remind him that God could have crushed him at any moment. We cannot stand against His power and might. Instead, we must be careful to bow to His holiness, even in those times that we wrestle with Him for blessings in our lives.

Read Psalm 105:1-11.

The first five verses of this passage instruct us to do the following things: give thanks to the Lord; call on His name; make known what He has done; sing praises; tell of His wonderful acts; glory in His name; rejoice; look to the Lord; seek His face; and remember His miracles.

Sometimes when we are struggling with our circumstances or with the Lord, it can be extremely difficult to give thanks, sing and rejoice. When we do not understand or comprehend God's plan, we often turn away from Him rather than looking to His face.

But, I have found that when I take the time to remember what God has done for me in the past, that it gives me the courage and strength to trust Him in the present and to cling to Him for whatever may come in the days ahead. When I remember what He has done for me, I am able to give thanks, call on Him, tell of His wonders, sing praises, rejoice and seek His face. When I am reminded of the Lord's great power and might and how He has displayed it in my life, I am able to turn to Him, to look to Him and to put my hope in the promises of His word.

Although it may not always appear evident, God is a good God, and He loves us. He wants the absolute best for our lives. No matter what your circumstances might be today, hold on to God. Be like Jacob, and don't let go of the Lord!

DAY 24: MY MOMENT IN THE WILDERNESS

Write a prayer or some thoughts about today's Day in the Desert.

.

DAY 25: GOD OF GREAT PURPOSE

SCRIPTURE

So Joseph went after his brothers and found them near Dothan. But they saw him in the distance, and before he reached them, they plotted to kill him.

So when Joseph came to his brothers, they stripped him of his robe—the richly ornamented robe he was wearing—and they took him and threw him into the cistern. Now the cistern was empty; there was no water in it.

So when the Midianite merchants came by, his brothers pulled Joseph up out of the cistern and sold him for twenty shekels of silver to the Ishmaelites, who took him to Egypt.

Genesis 37:17b, 23-24

Joseph said to his brothers, "I am Joseph! Is my father still living?" But his brothers were not able to answer him, because they were terrified at his presence.

Then Joseph said to his brothers, "Come close to me." When they had done so, he said, "I am your brother Joseph, the one you sold into Egypt! And now, do not be distressed and do not be angry with yourselves for selling me here, because it was to save lives that God sent me ahead of you."

Genesis 45:3-5

JESUS PRAYS

God of Great Purpose,

Does the enemy lurk around me, still seeking to bring Me to utter ruin; to harm Me completely? For does he not know; has he not heard; is he not aware that it is through harm that the lives of many shall be saved? Oh, how he wastes his time—how his purpose is carried out in vain. For though he sell Me for thirty silver pieces, he shall not gain at all. In trading Me for earthly loot, he shall purchase his eternal doom. Oh, that he would see and understand that his deeds will not prevail; that he would humble himself with fear and awe at the majesty of God. But, to Your plan he will never surrender. For he finds the thought of bowing to another an act beneath his will. And rather than proclaim the glory of the King of kings, he aims to take the Holy throne. Yet, on that day when every knee shall bow and every tongue confess, he will tremble in fear. For, he will know that You are magnificent and regal—that You are the King eternal, and he will be terrified at Your greatness.

Much like the day when Joseph's brothers learned that he was the ruler of all Egypt. O, how they trembled at his presence—afraid of what he might do to them because of their cruelty. For, jealousy drove them to sell Joseph into slavery. Yet, even through their atrocious act, a heavenly purpose still prevailed. For, You knew that twenty years later he would deliver his brothers from famine and death. Even in the midst of unfair circumstances, a greater purpose was served. For, You chose the outcome; You wrote the whole story—and You controlled the end.

Therefore, what Joseph said to his brothers, I now speak to the enemy, *"So then, it was not you who sent Me here, but God"* (Genesis 45:8).

Father, no doubt invades My mind, because I know this wilderness meeting is a wonderful moment in Your well-designed plan.

I know that like Joseph, I will be thrown into a pit; I will be sold and betrayed, falsely accused and murdered. Yet, even still, I echo the words of Joseph when I say to the enemy, *"Am I in the place of God? You intended to harm me, but God intended it for good to accomplish what is now being done, the saving of many lives"* (Genesis 50:19-20).

Jesus

DAY 25: A DAY IN THE DESERT

Read Genesis 50:15-21.

What a happy ending to such a dreadfully sad story. Joseph dealt with a lot of setbacks in his life. He was sold into slavery by his jealous brothers, falsely accused of rape, thrown into prison and forgotten. Yet, God used all of the difficult circumstances in his life for a greater good, and Joseph was used years later to save his brothers' lives.

Read Genesis 45:4-8.

Joseph must have had an enormous faith in God. For only a person with an intimate relationship with the Father could have the attitude of Joseph. How many of us, when we are wronged (especially by our closest family members and friends) have a forgiving spirit like Joseph? He could have chosen to harm his brothers; to pay them back for their cruelty, but, instead, he forgave them and then went so far as to encourage them! Can you believe it? Listen again to his words, *"...do not be angry with yourselves for selling me here, because it was to save lives that God sent me ahead of you....God sent me ahead of you to preserve for you a remnant on earth and to save your lives by a great deliverance"* (Genesis 45:5, 7).

I find that story simply incredible! Joseph was sent ahead of his brothers, to be placed in a position of power and authority, so that he could be instrumental in saving the lives of many people during the years of famine. Truly, I marvel at God and His sovereignty.

I am amazed at the story of Joseph, but the story of Jesus Christ simply baffles my mind. Do you ever just stop and think about the fact that Jesus came to earth so that our lives would be saved? God sent Jesus to save our lives by a "great deliverance." It wasn't an accident. It was purposeful! A price had to be paid for our sins, and Jesus was sent to pay that price with His life.

Do you understand the gift we have been given? Do you comprehend the love story that exists between you and God? Long before you and I were ever born, God sent Someone ahead of us, so that in our time of need, we could be saved.

Jesus endured some dreadful days for us. Did it ever occur to you that the days Jesus spent in the wilderness were not relaxing? He wasn't on a vacation—just camping out under the stars. He was sent into the wilderness to be *"tested by the devil"* (Matthew 4:1). He wasn't on a nature walk! Did you ever think about the fact that Jesus could have called it quits in that dusty region? He could have simply given up. Before the week of His arrest; before the inquiries and beatings; before He was mocked and spat upon, Jesus could have said, "No!"

Maybe we don't pay attention to the things that happened while Jesus was in the wilderness for forty days because the Bible doesn't give us all of the details of exactly what took place there. But, maybe we skim over that short passage in the Bible because we don't want to pause long enough to think about the fact that Jesus suffered for you and me. It is simply heartbreaking to know that He suffered on the cross for us; and that pain is magnified for me when I think about the fact that Jesus probably knew during His desert days that His journey would lead Him to the crucifixion. What amazes me even more is that He chose to keep going. He chose to hold on to God's plan. He chose to be placed in harm's way so that my life could be saved!

What a happy ending!

DAY 25: MY MOMENT IN THE WILDERNESS

Write a prayer or some thoughts about today's Day in the Desert.

DAY 26: MY PURPOSE WILL STAND

～⚬⚬～

GOD SPEAKS

My Son,

My purpose will stand, and I will do all that I please.

God

DAY 26: A DAY IN THE DESERT

When I am having a bad day, and I vent to my mother, I love to hear her say, "You'll be strong."

When I have a bad dream, and I wake up in a fright, I love to hear my husband whisper, "You're okay. I'm here."

When life gets difficult and suffering is at hand, I love to hear my Savior say:

So do not fear, for I am with you; do not be dismayed, for I am your God, I will strengthen you and help you; I will uphold you with my righteous right hand (Isaiah 41:10).

When things are confusing and I just do not understand why things happen as they do, I love to hear God say:

Do you not know? Have you not heard? The Lord is the everlasting God, the Creator of the ends of the earth. He will not grow tired or weary, and his understanding no one can fathom. He gives strength to the weary and increases the power of the weak (Isaiah 40:28-29).

A comfort in times of trouble; that is what God is to me. He gives me peace, even when I do not comprehend His plan. He brings me joy, even when there is pain in the circumstances of life. He is my hope; my constant; my steady. He is even, continuous and faithful.

Read Isaiah 46:10.

Do you believe God's purpose will stand?

Read Acts 5:12-42.

What a wonderful story of God fulfilling His purpose! The apostles were jailed, only to be released by an angel of the Lord. They were questioned and threatened, only to proclaim that they would obey God rather than men. The high priest and his associates wanted to kill the apostles, only to be convinced by a Pharisee to spare their lives. The apostles were beaten and told to quit speaking in the name of Jesus, but *"they never stopped teaching and proclaiming the good news that Jesus is the Christ"* (Acts 5:42).

God's plan stood the test. One of my favorite parts of this story is when Gamaliel said,

> *Leave these men alone! Let them go! For if their purpose or activity is of human origin, it will fail. But if it is from God, you will not be able to stop these men; you will only find yourselves fighting against God* (Acts 5:39).

For, you see, Peter and the other apostles prevailed; they never quit. And, it is because of their willingness to tell others the good news of Christ that I heard the story! The message was passed down from generation to generation because God planned for the people in this world to know Christ and to be saved!

I would venture to say that when Jesus was in the wilderness He probably did not need a reminder that God's purpose would stand; I'm sure He knew that fact full well. However, if God really did speak the words *"My purpose will stand, and I will do all that I please,"* He probably spoke them in the context of comfort—as if He was saying, "You'll be strong" or "You're okay. I'm here."

A comfort in times of trouble is what God is. He gives peace. He brings joy. He is hope. I have no doubt that His plan will stand.

DAY 26: MY MOMENT IN THE WILDERNESS

Write a prayer or some thoughts about today's Day in the Desert.

DAY 27: MIGHTY SPIRIT OF GOD

SCRIPTURE

Now the Lord had said to Moses, "I will bring one more plague on Pharaoh and on Egypt. After that, he will let you go from here, and when he does, he will drive you out completely."

So Moses said, "This is what the Lord says: 'About midnight I will go throughout Egypt. Every firstborn son in Egypt will die, from the firstborn son of Pharaoh, who sits on the throne, to the firstborn son of the slave girl, who is at her hand mill, and all the firstborn of the cattle as well. There will be loud wailing throughout Egypt—worse than there has ever been or ever will be again. But among the Israelites not a dog will bark at any man or animal. Then you will know that the Lord makes a distinction between Egypt and Israel.'"

The Lord had said to Moses, "Pharaoh will refuse to listen to you—so that my wonders may be multiplied in Egypt."

Exodus 11:1, 4-7, 9

JESUS PRAYS

Mighty Spirit of God,

Iawoke to the sound of a doe this morning as it cried out for its young now lost. The sound so full of agony, so laced with pain — it moves My being. How I long to join this mother on her quest to find her young. Such cries remind Me of days gone by in the land of Egypt. O, Spirit, do You remember? Can You still hear the sound of hearts breaking? Do the wails of the Egyptians still echo through the walls of glory? In that moment when the breath of life was taken — the moment of time when You, Holy Spirit, passed over the Israelites yet sucked the life out of the Egyptian firstborn — O, there was a wailing so deep, so loud, so piercing — and it moves Me to this day. I shall never forget that sound.

Yet, in this very moment, as I face the stark barrenness of this place, I am reminded of the hush that fell over the Israelites in the seconds You passed by. Not even a dog opened his mouth to bark at Your presence — for Your power stilled two nations living in one land. O, Father, how Your mercy and judgment were revealed in the midst of Your Spirit's movement as You permeated the land of Egypt. And, although My heart rejoices at the rescue of Your people Israel, I ache at the memory of Your judgment. I am saddened by Pharaoh's refusal to listen to You through Your servant Moses. His heart was so cold, so calloused, so hard. He was immovable and stubborn until broken by Your Spirit; for he, too, lost his firstborn son. He, too, was devastated by Your passing judgment.

And, nothing has changed. For even though You carried the Israelites to the Promised Land, Your people are still hard at heart. They are still so cold, so calloused. Therefore, I must be in this land — I must suffer; I must die. For an impending moment of judgment will come in the days ahead. So, O God, let Me be the unblemished Lamb. Spill My blood. Sacrifice Me for the sins of man. Father, take My life, take My blood — place it over the door and the sides of man's heart. Cover him with mercy so that Your Spirit of judgment will pass over him, and he will be saved. For I love Your people, O

God, and, I long to be the instrument of salvation that will atone for man's sins.

Yet, I am tempted in this place God. I am tempted to quit and to leave this land. For days are beginning to run into days. I feel as though I have been here a lifetime, yet I know only weeks have passed Me by. O Father, do You hear Me as I cry out to You? Are You listening as My heart breaks? Do the wails of Your Son echo through the walls of glory? For You know when the mountain goats give birth. You watch when the doe bears her fawn. You count the months till they bear. You know the time they give birth. They crouch down and bring forth their young; their labor pains are ended. Their young thrive and grow strong in the wilds; they leave and do not return. And even now, as this mother doe calls out for her young, You hear. You see. You respond. Just as You responded to the cries of the Israelites. Just as You respond to Me. For I know My suffering in the wilderness pales in comparison to the glory that will be revealed through My life. Even now You are perfecting My humanness as I go through this temptation trial. My heart, O Father, shall not grow hard. I shall not become cold and calloused. For, I will remain moldable and useful in Your hands. Come to Me now, My Father. Do not pass Me by, O Spirit.

Jesus

DAY 27: A DAY IN THE DESERT

Can you imagine the pain of the Egyptian families? Why did God have to go to such drastic measures? Why did Pharaoh's hardened heart have to affect the entire people of Egypt? Things like this I certainly can't understand; they are mysteries to me. However, I know that God is in control. When I find myself struggling to grasp God's ways, I take comfort in the words Moses spoke to the Israelites in Deuteronomy 29:29 when he said: *"The secret things belong to the Lord our God, but the things revealed belong to us and to our children forever, that we may follow all the words of this law."*

Those words sure do take the pressure off! What a relief! I do not have to know everything about God! I simply need to follow the things He has revealed to me in His word and remember that His thoughts are so much greater than mine.

The Bible tells us that no one can fathom the greatness of God. Even if we try with all of our own intellect, we are still unable to take in all of God's magnitude.

Read Isaiah 55:8-9 and Psalm 145:3.

As we read the letters of Paul, we find that he received the gospel through divine revelation. In Romans he tells us that God revealed His mystery to us so that we would believe and obey Him. Salvation is not a secret! God does not leave us guessing about His love for us.

Read Romans 16:25-27 and Ephesians 1:7-10.

God revealed the purpose of His divine mystery to Paul so that the gospel could be proclaimed to the Gentiles.

Read Colossians 1:25-27 and Romans 15:7-12.

Paul was used by God to fulfill a prophecy and promise which was spoken to the Israelite patriarchs—Abraham, Isaac and Jacob. When God sent the plagues to Egypt, when His Spirit moved over the land and took all of the firstborn, He was rescuing His chosen people. God was moving them to a land of promise and freedom so that years later the Gentiles could hear the wonderful message of the Exodus and put their faith in a God who saves. God planned for all people to know and recognize Him as the true and faithful God. And, although I will never fully understand the big picture of that first Passover moment, I am grateful that God spared the Israelites; and, I am thankful that the mysterious message of salvation has been brought to light so that all men may believe and obey God.

DAY 27: MY MOMENT IN THE WILDERNESS

Write a prayer or some thoughts about today's Day in the Desert.

DAY 28: ALMIGHTY GOD

SCRIPTURE

During the last watch of the night the Lord looked down from the pillar of fire and cloud at the Egyptian army and threw it into confusion.

Exodus 14:24

JESUS PRAYS

Almighty God,

Why must they harden their hearts? Why, even though rescued and protected, must they turn away—relying upon their own understanding? How quickly Your people forget. Will they forget Me too? Will their hearts even recognize the sacrifice? Will they even believe? This suffering is for them—will they even care?

O, the lengths that You have taken in order to save Your people. Yet they still doubt. Even after deliverance from Egypt they voiced their questions; they cried out in bitter unbelief. How their hearts tricked them—for they believed their exodus was a walk unto death rather than a freedom march. But, O how Your servant Moses proclaimed truth! I remember how his voice thundered through heaven when he said to the Israelites:

Do not be afraid. Stand firm and you will see the deliverance the Lord will bring you today. The Egyptians you see today you will never see again. The Lord will fight for you; you need only to be still (Exodus 14:13).

His words hushed heaven itself. For we knew Your power would soon be displayed. And as You blew a strong wind from the east, the walls of heaven rumbled. As You stretched out Your hand over the sea, we stood in amazement at Your might. And, as the water gave way to dry ground we began to shout hallelujahs to Your name. For we knew Your glory would be revealed.

Woe to those who go down to Egypt for help, who rely on horses, who trust in the multitude of their chariots and in the great strength of their horsemen, but do not look to the Holy One of Israel, or seek help from the Lord....the Egyptians are men and not God; their horses are flesh and not spirit. When the Lord stretches out his hand, he who helps will stumble, he who is helped will fall; both will perish together (Isaiah 31:1-3).

And perish they did! O, how the Egyptians trusted in horses and chariots—how they believed in the strength of animals and in the might of armies. Yet when they entered the floor of the sea to pursue Your people, the water flowed back and covered them. You blew with Your breath, and the best of Pharaoh's officers were drowned in the Red Sea. They sank like lead in the mighty waters, and when the Israelites witnessed Your great power, they feared You and put their trust in You! And, then heaven erupted in praise!

And now, I stand upon this dry ground—arms outstretched—hands lifted high. And though My enemy pursue Me, I will lift My alleluias to Your name. For no one is more powerful than You! I shout to You, O God! I raise My voice in thunderous praise—My joyful battle cries ring out across this barren land and reverberate upon the rocks on which I stand. And even when Your people remember Me not, I will proclaim Your name.

For You are My strength and My song. Your right hand is majestic—for with Your right hand You will shatter My enemy; You will throw down the one who opposes Me. You will unleash Your anger against him and consume him like stubble. What a wonder You are!

Jesus

DAY 28: A DAY IN THE DESERT

My five year old nephew is quite an independent little fellow. Like most youngsters, he wants to do everything himself. He likes to open and close the door to the car all alone. And, if you forget and accidentally close the door for him, he opens it and closes it "all by himself." He is learning how to put puzzles together, and I am quite impressed with his diligence. He will work and work until all of the pieces fit together just perfectly. But, should you try to place a piece into the puzzle, he will remove it and put it back "all by himself."

You may not remember all the little antics you went through as a young child, but most of us were probably at lot like my nephew — just discovering the world, our gifts, our abilities. And, at such a young age, we were already growing into our own independence. Even though we still needed help, we liked to do things "all by ourselves."

Most of us are so blessed with gifts, skills and abilities that we often fall into a trap of trusting in ourselves. We grow so self-sufficient, depending on our money, talent, position and power that we forget to place our lives into the steady care of the Lord. The danger comes when we begin to trust in our own plans. When we have an "I'll do it my way" mentality, we lose sight of the fact that we really do need God; we really do need His help.

The Bible tells us in Isaiah that the Egyptians trusted in the power of their horses and chariots, the strength of their armies, rather than trusting in the Lord. Their refusal to trust God led to their ruin.

Read Psalm 33:16-22.

In the case of the Egyptians, it did not matter the size of the army or the strength of the horses — nothing could stand against the Lord's might. He is so great. And, even though He has blessed us with positions of power, we will never grow stronger than the Lord. As we hope in Him, rather than trusting in our own independence, we are delivered from harm. The Lord truly is our help and our shield. Our salvation does not come from ourselves; it comes from God.

Read Proverbs 11:28 and Proverbs 28:26.

When we trust in riches and in ourselves, we will fall. But, when we live in righteousness and when we make decisions with wisdom, we will thrive and be kept safe.

Do you trust God? Do you trust Him in your job situations, or do you make decisions without God's help? Are you so talented and educated in your field that you don't think you need God's guidance? Have you entered into a relationship without trusting God for advice? Are you trusting in your own intellect, talents or beauty to give you the success and happiness you seek in this life? If so, what will be the outcome of your experiences? Will you truly know the power of God in your life? Will you know true satisfaction, peace and security? Or, will you trust in your own abilities and dread the day that your strength runs out? What happens when that more intelligent, better looking, more educated person comes into your work place? Will you suddenly find yourself fighting to keep everything you have worked so hard to obtain?

Read the following verses:

Psalm 40:4
Proverbs 16:20
Proverbs 3:5-6
Psalm 20:7
Psalm 37:3-6

Where do you place your trust?

DAY 28: MY MOMENT IN THE WILDERNESS

Are you placing your trust in another human being; in your bank account; or in yourself?

Write a prayer asking God for the strength and courage to trust Him completely, or write some thoughts about today's Day in the Desert.

DAY 29: NO SAVIOR APART FROM ME

GOD SPEAKS

My Child,

Before Me no god was formed, nor will there be one after Me. I, even I, am the LORD, and apart from Me there is no Savior.

God

DAY 29: A DAY IN THE DESERT

Do you believe God's claim? His word tells us that there is no Savior apart from Him. Many people accept that there are multiple ways to God; that the various religions in our world today all point to one God, and as long as people are devout in their own religion, then they will go to heaven.

Read Isaiah 43:10-13.

In this passage the Israelites are serving as God's witnesses to His saving power. All of the things that God has done to rescue His people from bondage, harm and destruction are examples of His redemption and grace. When you read through the Bible, you again see the evidence of God's salvation. None of the foreign gods are able to rescue, redeem or save the Israelites from ruin, but our God saves.

The world we live in today is not too terribly different from the ancient world, from the world as it was when Christ lived on earth or from the days when Paul tried to spread the truth of the gospel. From the beginning of time, people have been deceived into believing that God is not who He says He is. False prophets have been trying to turn the hearts of God's people away from the truth since the days of creation. Satan disguised himself as an instrument of truth in the Garden, and he masqueraded himself as an angel of light during the days of Paul. Today, he imitates all wisdom and knowledge as he sprinkles the truth with lies and replaces faith with doubt. He manipulates and confuses wise men; convincing them that intelligence is power and insight into self is the way of salvation. He is wrong.

Read Matthew 7:15-20; 24:11; 24:24.

Jesus warned us about false prophets. Paul preached against Satan's servants. The word of God sheds light on the fact that a counterfeit religion would try to take the place of true salvation through Jesus Christ. As Christians we need to know the truth. We need to be reminded that Jesus Christ is the only way we can have salvation from our sins and know eternal life.

Read Galatians 1:6-9.

Even in early New Testament days, false prophets were trying to confuse the true message of Christ by teaching that some of the ceremonial practices of the Old Testament were still necessary for salvation (circumcision being one of these necessities). Paul continually preached that salvation was through grace. In Galatians 2, Paul states:

A man is not justified by observing the law, but by faith in Jesus Christ. So we, too, have put our faith in Christ Jesus that we may be justified by faith in Christ and not by observing the law, because by observing the law no one will be justified (Galatians 2:15-16).

Read Luke 22:66-71.

Jesus claimed to be the Christ, God's Son. He knew by stating this truth that He would be sentenced to die because it was considered blasphemous to make such a declaration. Yet, He still proclaimed to be the Messiah.

In Mark 15:33-39 we read the account of Jesus breathing His last breath. A centurion, who watched the entire event take place proclaimed, *"Surely this man was the Son of God"* (Mark 15:39).

As Christians, we are God's witnesses—just as the Israelites were His witnesses in days of old, and the centurion was a witness at the foot of the cross. We need to proclaim that Jesus is the Son of God so that those in this world who are confused and deceived may hear the truth and receive God's grace in their lives. If you believe God's claim—that apart from Him there is no Savior—then what is keeping you from telling others the truth?

DAY 29: MY MOMENT IN THE WILDERNESS

Write a prayer or some thoughts about today's Day in the Desert.

DAY 30: MAGNIFICENT GOD

SCRIPTURE

"Blessed is she who has believed that what the Lord has said to her will be accomplished!"

Luke 1:45

JESUS PRAYS

Magnificent God,

I miss my mother today God. What a beautiful woman, what a beautiful face. How I dread the pain she will soon suffer. O, that she should be spared the horror of sacrifice. I know that her life fits into Your plan; I rest assured that she will be cared for when I am gone. I truly do long to keep her from harm, and yet I know that just as the temple curtain will be torn, her heart will be ripped in two. I know the answer before I even speak the question, but even still I shall ask for Your Spirit to comfort her heart and to give her quick understanding. For You found her favorable long ago and sent Your angel to her to announce My coming. And Mary said, *"I am the Lord's servant. May it be to me as you have said"* (Luke 1:38).

May she forever remember the words to the song she once sang, *"My soul glorifies the Lord and my spirit rejoices in God my Savior, for he has been mindful of the humble state of his servant"* (Luke

1:46-48). Father, even in the midst of what she will witness, may she remember You and take heart in Your Word. For I know that from the moment of My birth announcement until now that she has watched, listened, questioned and pondered—treasuring and storing all these things in her heart. Yet God, I know that You have been preparing her from the beginning. For on the eighth day of My life, You made her aware of my death when Simeon spoke these words to her:

> *This child is destined to cause the falling and rising of many in Israel, and to be a sign that will be spoken against, so that the thoughts of many hearts will be revealed. And a sword will pierce your own soul too* (Luke 2:34-35).

And though at that very moment she did not grasp the full reality, I know she caught a glimpse of something beyond her understanding. For I am confident that her soul is sensitive to the truth; she knows full well that I am the Messiah even though she does not fully comprehend Your ways. Thank you for preparing her heart.

My dear mother. I will never forget the time we traveled to Jerusalem for the Feast of the Passover; my parents and family began their journey home while I visited the temple. Father, I was drawn to You. Even as a young boy of twelve, I was eager to listen, learn and teach others about You and Your truth. O, My poor mother. The look on her face when she found Me was one of terror and fright mixed with sheer relief. For I know she was so worried at the thought of losing Me; so frantic that I could not be found among the traveling caravan. Even then how I wished she could have understood that I was in My Father's house—the temple—doing His work. For then she would have known to look within the temple immediately; she would have known My whereabouts. Yet, upon returning home that day, and throughout subsequent days, as I grew in wisdom and stature, and in favor with God and man, My mother treasured everything in her heart. She could sense the power of God in My life, and she began to firmly believe. Even still, there will be moments when I know she will fear for My life—when religious men grow suspicious and jealous and plot to kill Me; when crowds gather around Me so tight and so often that I will forego food and rest. In those moments I know My precious mother will do her very best to protect Me and watch over Me. Remind her, heavenly Father, that I am the Lord and no weapon formed against Me shall stand. Fill her with a sense of firm belief and courage as she endures the episodes of My life. And provide her with strength as she tries to understand the mysteries of her son — the Son of God.

Jesus

DAY 30: A DAY IN THE DESERT

All of us have seen them—the "My child is an honor student" bumper stickers, or the soccer balls, mega phones and basketball stickers with little Johnny and little Susie's names printed across them. Let's face it, we are proud parents.

In the town where I live there is an interesting tradition. Two weeks before the seniors graduate, friends and family make banners and hang them on a fence across the street from the school. Some banners are handmade; some are printed professionally. Each banner bears the name of a graduate along with words of congratulation. Many banners have oversized photographs of the graduating senior. Let's face it, we are proud parents.

Read Luke 2:41-52.

I wonder what other emotions accompanied Mary and Joseph when they found twelve year old Jesus in the temple. The Bible says in Luke that they were "astonished." Could they have been proud as well? Maybe, if bumper stickers were popular in that day, their's would have read, "My child taught in the temple courts." Or, if banners were a tradition, they would have draped one over a camel on their way back home; it might have pictured Jesus sitting among the teachers of the temple, as he listened and asked questions. Mary and Joseph must have known that there was something very special about Jesus.

Maybe on that long walk home they thought back to the day Jesus was presented in the temple. He was only eight days old when Simeon, a righteous man, saw Christ.

Read Luke 2:25-33.

Although prophecy had already been pronounced to Mary and Joseph about Christ, they still marveled at each new revelation. They were still astonished at the things they heard. I am sure Jesus was just as amazing to them as He is to us today. God, in the flesh, dwelt among them. He lived in their home. He ate dinner at their table. They broke bread with the Bread of Life. It must have been awesome. And, in those moments when they stopped to consider the reality in their midst, I am sure they were overwhelmed with the fact that salvation rested in the hands and heart of their child. He, indeed, was the Messiah, and He would change the world.

Read Isaiah 11:1, 10.

These verses prophesy Jesus Christ, the Messiah. He is the banner of love and salvation for our lives.

Read Psalm 20:4-5.

If someone made a banner for me today, I would hope that it would reflect the message found in Psalm 20:4-5. As my life is displayed for the world, I want to be a banner lifted high in the name of God that it may draw many to Christ. I do not simply want my name displayed for the sake of pride or to highlight my mere achievements. I desire for my life to make a statement of honor for the One who deserves all praise—His name is Jesus. How marvelous.

What about you? Do you still marvel? Are you astonished and amazed that the Spirit of the Living God has made a home in your heart? When you stop to consider what Christ has done for you, are you awestruck? Is your life a banner for the Lord? Are you proud to know the Child of God? Will you display Him in your actions, words and deeds?

DAY 30: MY MOMENT IN THE WILDERNESS

What is written on the banner of your life? Write a prayer asking God to help you display His love and grace to others, or write some thoughts about today's Day in the Desert.

DAY 31: GOD OF ISRAEL'S ARMIES

―♋♋―

SCRIPTURE

David said to the Philistine, "You come against me with sword and spear and javelin, but I come against you in the name of the Lord Almighty, the God of Israel, whom you have defied."

As the Philistine moved closer to attack him, David ran quickly toward the battle line to meet him.

1 Samuel 17:45, 48

JESUS PRAYS

God of Israel's Armies,

O how I marvel at the courage and strength of King David. Even as a young man, untrained in battle, he was not afraid to stand before his enemy and fight. And, not only did he fight, be he ran quickly towards his foe—with full confidence that You would be his defender; that You would be the Victor in the battle. I remember the scene so very well. In fact, I was on the edge of My throne as I peered onto the battlefield. Goliath stood over nine feet tall; his armor and weapons of iron and bronze intimidated all of

185

Saul's army. Not a single man would take on the giant and silence his incessant heckling. Instead, they all ran away from Goliath; fear filled their hearts and minds.

But not young David. He was quite the opposite exactly. Fear did not accompany the shepherd boy. Instead, he welcomed the opportunity to oppose the one who defied the Almighty God. Such a glorious chorus filled the chambers of heaven when the angels heard David say, *"The Lord who delivered me from the paw of the lion and the paw of the bear will deliver me from the hand of this Philistine"* (1 Samuel 17:37). They sang songs of praise and deliverance as they glorified Your name throughout the kingdom. Nothing moves Me more than those who put their trust in You. *"Those who know your name will trust in you, for you, Lord, have never forsaken those who seek you"* (Psalm 9:10).

David had every confidence that You would defend Your name; You would destroy the one who stood against You. How beautiful were the words the young boy spoke to the Philistine:

You come against me with sword and spear and javelin, but I come against you in the name of the Lord Almighty, the God of the armies of Israel, whom you have defied. This day the Lord will hand you over to me, and I'll strike you down and cut off your head (1 Samuel 17:45-46a).

David trusted in Your name. And, I too, trust in the name of My God. For I know that You are My Deliverer. Just as David ran towards his opponent, may the dust stir under My feet as I run into the face of My foe. Move My feet with swift confidence as I engage the enemy in battle. And though he comes at Me with weapons of death and destruction, I know that the battle is the Lord's. The enemy will be given over into My hand, and on that day the angels will once again sing songs of praise and deliverance throughout the kingdom.

Jesus

DAY 31: A DAY IN THE DESERT

My niece is fearless. She chases after adventure. As a toddler, she climbed to the top of my brother's Jeep and waved at everyone; the smile on her face wider than the Mississippi River. Seeing her on the top of that vehicle scared me, but she was having the time of her life. When she was four, she climbed a rock wall that most adults would refuse to climb. Of course, I stood at the foot of the wall cheering for her; both of my feet firmly planted on the ground. She is an inspiration to me. When I spend time with her, I am always infected by her fun, outgoing, adventuresome spirit. She makes me laugh, and in her presence I am reminded that our moments should be lived with confidence and joy instead of with anxiety and fear.

Read 1 Samuel 17.

There are many amazing things about this particular story in David's life; however, in my opinion, one of the most remarkable truths is that David **ran** *towards* Goliath. Great day! Where was the fear? As we can see it was absolutely non-existent. David was so full of confidence in God's power that he actually pursued his enemy. He knew that victory was his for the taking, and he was not about to back down. He defeated Goliath.

Think about the enemies in your life. What are the giants that you are facing in your life today; the things that are standing against God; the things that mock your belief system; the things that defy the almighty power of God? Are you in the middle of a battle?

Are your aging in-laws zapping you of the strength you need to just maintain some level of normalcy? Are you standing before a mountain of debt, knowing that the mortgage payment is due tomorrow? Has the doctor just recently given you the news that the biopsy confirmed his suspicions of cancer? Are you placing all of your hope in the last and final fertility treatment?

Often, life comes at us with sword and spear and javelin; however, as Christians, we have the power of the Almighty God on our side. And, we do not have to give way to fear in our lives.

Read the following verses:

Psalm 23:4
Psalm 27:1
Psalm 46:2
Psalm 91:4-5
Proverbs 1:33
Proverbs 29:25
Isaiah 35:3-4

Throughout the Bible, God reminds us not to fear. He reassures us that His presence is a constant in our lives, and that we are surrounded by His divine protection. We will all suffer in some form or another as we travel through the days of this life; however, we do not have to endure our circumstances in a state of fear. Instead, we can embrace the days of our lives with the confidence of young David, and we can run after the things that threaten us.

Ironically, in 1 Samuel 17:51 we read, *"When the Philistines saw that their hero was dead, they turned and ran."* David ran towards a fearful situation; the Philistines ran away.

In which way are you running? Are you facing the fear in your life with confidence, or are you running away from the things that you need to confront?

DAY 31: MY MOMENT IN THE WILDERNESS

Today, write about some of the things that you fear in your life. Ask God to help you to remember that the battle belongs to Him, or write some thoughts about today's Day in the Desert.

DAY 32: ARMED WITH STRENGTH

—⟅ↄ ⟅ↄ—

GOD SPEAKS

My Son,

I have armed You with strength and made Your way perfect.

God

DAY 32: A DAY IN THE DESERT

What tempts you? For the alcoholic, is it the couple sitting next to you drinking a glass of wine? Or, is it the smell of cigarettes that triggers a once forgotten habit? Are you tempted to yell back when you know it is better to keep a tight rein on your tongue? Does the extra dessert send you into bliss or regret? Do you keep late hours at work because the conversation there makes you feel better than the nagging you receive at home? Are you trying to make the sports team at school, so you sneak a peek at a classmate's test answer? Does the rush of just one more roll of the dice keep you betting away your savings account? Do you long for love in the arms of someone who doesn't belong to you? Are you tired of waiting to be married before you enjoy the act of sex? Do you want the promotion enough to compromise your integrity? Have beauty secrets and diets become your sense of identity? Do you have to follow the latest trend, buy the cute dress before she does so that you are noticed first? What tempts you?

Read 1 Corinthians 10:13.

Have you ever thought about the fact that God will provide a way for you to stand up under temptation? Take comfort in knowing that all of us have been tempted in some form or another, and rejoice in the fact that Jesus Christ understands temptation.

Read Hebrews 2:18.

The temptation of Jesus is not a fable; He really did suffer for us.

Read Hebrews 4:14-16.

Jesus, although tempted, never sinned; He never disobeyed God or chose to do things on His own rather than trusting God. He is our perfect example. We know, of course, that we will not ever be perfect; however, we can take comfort in knowing that Jesus sympathizes with us because He has experienced temptation.

When we are tempted, we can look to Christ and follow His lead. He combated lies with the truth of God's word. He chose to believe the promises of God rather than accepting the counterfeit deal. Jesus did not bow down to Satan because He was already submitted to the Father.

Read James 4:7-8.

As Christians we have the power to overcome! When our lives are submitted to Christ, we have the strength to resist the devil. Psalm 18:32 says, *"It is God who arms me with strength and makes my way perfect."* The Bible tells us that when we stand against the schemes of Satan, that he will flee from us. Don't be afraid of the devil *"because the one who is in you is greater than the one who is in the world"* (1 John 4:4).

What tempts you? Submit your heart to God, stand firm, and watch the devil flee.

DAY 32: MY MOMENT IN THE WILDERNESS

Write a prayer asking God to help you flee from temptation, or write some thoughts about today's Day in the Desert.

DAY 33: GOD OF THE LOWLY

—⟨⟩⟨⟩—

SCRIPTURE

Here is a trustworthy saying: If we died with him, we will also live with him; if we endure, we will also reign with him. If we disown him, he will also disown us; if we are faithless, he will remain faithful, for he cannot disown himself.

2 Timothy 2:11-13

JESUS PRAYS

God of the Lowly,

To You, God, everything matters—even things which seem insignificant—those things of little value to the worldly masses are close to Your heart—the forsaken widow, the fatherless child, the forgotten prisoner. You are a good and faithful God, forgetting no one. Even now in this place of loneliness, You remember Me. As My mother, father, brothers and cousins hustle about the city involved in the busyness of their lives they may seldom think of Me. Yet, Your Spirit led Me here to this quiet place of abandonment for a divine appointment. And although human companionship may be far from Me, I am wrapped in the reality of the holy friendship and unity that exists between us. I rest assured that Your thoughts towards Me are fond and forever. At this moment I may be obscure to the world—a stranger, a simple carpenter's son, a Nazarene—but to You I am the crux of Your plan, the climax of Your redemptive story rests with Me. And although My name is commonplace today, it shall be renown in future days. For to You, O God, everything matters—even an axhead. For who but You could defy the laws of gravity? Who but You could place a wooden stick into a body of water and cause iron to float? Only You, My God. Only You. And why? What moves You to rescue an unknown prophet in the company of many? Why do You care about a seemingly insignificant person in society—one with no means to pay for an ax—one who would become a bondservant in order to pay off the loss of a borrowed axhead. How enormous is Your love for those in need; how wide is the spread of Your mercy to the ones the world erases. You, however, highlight the faithful; You pour Your goodness on the broken, downtrodden, desperate. You are not a forgetful God—for You remember the ones this world discards. You help those in a prison of hopeless thought, in the chains of unbelief, behind the bars of disappointment. You run after those who live alone.

Blessed is he whose help is the God of Jacob, whose hope is in the Lord his God, the Maker of heaven and earth, the sea and everything in them—the Lord, who remains faithful forever. He upholds the cause of the oppressed and gives food to the hungry. The Lord sets prisoners free, the Lord gives sight to the blind, the Lord lifts up those who are bowed down, the Lord loves the righteous. The Lord watches over the alien and sustains the fatherless and the widow, but he frustrates the ways of the wicked (Psalm 146:5-9).

Blessed are You, God. You remain faithful forever! You rescue the ones who cry out to the God, Most High. Everything matters to You, O God.

Jesus

DAY 33: A DAY IN THE DESERT

Read 2 Kings 6:1-7.

That God cared enough about a faithful servant to rescue him in time of need is so encouraging to me. I know there are times in my life when I panic and cry out to my God; just like the prophet cried, *"Oh, my lord, it was borrowed!"* There are times in my life when I have felt alone, nameless—like the only forgotten person on the planet—like my life has sunk below the ocean floor. But in those despairing moments, the Shepherd of my life steps into my circumstances and calls me by name, I recognize His voice, listen to Him and follow His lead—for the Good Shepherd laid down His life for me, and I am no longer insignificant.

When my life circumstances make me feel like I am going to sink to the bottom of an enormous body of water, I can cry out to God—knowing full well that He hears me and will rescue me. Praise the Lord for His long arm of love—that reaches us even when we are in the depths of pain and trouble. No dilemma is too perplexing for our Great God!

Do you ever feel forgotten, forsaken, alone? Is there a time when you recall feeling like you were invisible—as if no one even knew you existed? Remember, everything matters to God. Everyone matters. God cares about the details of your life, and He is there for you. Just as He cared about a nameless prophet's plight.

We do not know much about the prophet of 2 Kings 6. We don't know his name, his age or his social status. From Scripture, we can gather that he was one among a company or procession of prophets who traveled with Elisha. We can assume from his panic that he was not wealthy enough to afford an expensive axhead; therefore, he borrowed the tool. Obviously he was in distress at the idea of losing the item because he would probably be forced to become a slave in order to work off his debt.

Yet God, rich in mercy, prompted Elisha to cut a stick and throw it in the water. How amazing! God defied gravity and an iron axhead floats! The Bible does not record the man's response; however, I know I would have been relieved and overjoyed. I would have also been amazed at the display of power in the miracle Elisha performed. I might have been speechless, and my jaw might have dropped to the ground at the sight of the axhead atop the water, but I would have rejoiced! In fact, I might have grabbed the axhead and in my jubilation, I might have jumped up and down or twirled around in a victory dance! I would have been ecstatic! I would have probably made a bee line for the rightful owner and promptly returned his ax—grateful that I would not have been indebted to this man!

What about you? How would you respond? In fact, how do you respond when your life circumstances are heavy? What happens when your troubles seem to sink the life boat upon which you float? Do you cry out, "O Lord" or do you give up and drown in a sea of self-pity? Remember, everything matters to God. You matter to God.

DAY 33: MY MOMENT IN THE WILDERNESS

Write a prayer to God or some thoughts about today's Day in the Desert.

DAY 34: DO NOT FEAR

GOD SPEAKS

Jesus,

So do not fear, for I am with You; do not be dismayed, for I am Your God. I will strengthen You and help You; I will uphold You with My righteous right hand.

God

DAY 34: A DAY IN THE DESERT

Years ago when I was training for a race, my instructor would run a pace ahead of me. He would then reach back, grab my pinky finger and gently pull me. It may sound ridiculous, but that slight support gave me the strength that I needed to increase my pace. My instructor never left my side. When he noticed I was lagging, he would reach for my hand and pull me along. He was a beautiful picture of Christ to me.

Recently, a friend of mine and I were hiking up a steep hill. My hands were full, so I was having trouble balancing and making the climb at the same time. My friend placed her hand on my back and gave me a gentle push—steadying me and helping me at the same time. I immediately thought of God's right hand.

Sometimes the race is long and hard, and when we lag behind or feel like giving up, we can trust that our God is there to pull us along. At times the mountains in our lives seem too steep to climb, but our God is there to give us the gentle shove we need to make it to the top.

Read Isaiah 41:10.

God tells us not to fear because He promises to hold us up when times are difficult. Praise the Lord! However, trusting Him does not always come easy for some of us. When we are waiting for lab results, sometimes we fear. When the amount in the bank is less than the amount of the bill, sometimes we fear. When our children make poor choices; when our spouses don't call; when the refrigerator is bare, sometimes we fear.

Read Matthew 6:25-34.

Do you need God's steady hand today? Trust that He is there, and do not worry.

DAY 34: MY MOMENT IN THE WILDERNESS

What are you worrying about today? Write a prayer asking God to help you trust in Him rather than worrying about your circumstances, or write some thoughts about today's Day in the Desert.

DAY 35: THE ONE WHO PREVAILS

—༄ ༄—

SCRIPTURE

Great are the works of the Lord; they are pondered by all who delight in them. Glorious and majestic are his deeds, and his righteousness endures forever. He has caused his wonders to be remembered; the Lord is gracious and compassionate.

Psalm 111:2-4

JESUS PRAYS

The One Who Prevails,

My mind reflects today upon the schemes of the evil one. As I scan moments in days past I recognize his signature, his mark, his thumbprint upon plans which deviate from Your sovereign purpose. How ironic it is that he toils endlessly and yet he shall never know true victory. For with each passing day, he builds the instrument of his own demise—much like Haman in the days of King Xerxes. Haman's hatred for Mordecai and the Jewish people ultimately destroyed his life; just as My enemy's hatred of Me has set the course for his eternal doom.

All praise belongs to You, God, for even amidst an evil scheme You still prevail. For although Haman's plan to annihilate the Jews seemed imminent, You trumped his queen. For You strategically placed Esther and Mordecai into positions of influence and great power; knowing full well that they would be used to rescue the Jewish people from destruction. What seems to some as a circumstantial coincidence is indeed Your sovereignty at its best.

O, Father, how I long for mankind to realize the beauty of circumstances—that life is not a gamble, that things do happen for reasons unseen. O, that man could truly trust You instead of leaning on his own understandings. And, yet, he tries to reason and explain away the workings of the Almighty. O God, rescue man from himself; for, as he grows more tolerant of the world and its ways, he plays into Satan's conspiracy to annihilate the King and His followers. When man no longer adheres to Your absolute Truth, he becomes a pawn Satan can use to destroy the conscience, the heart, the soul.

And yet, when circumstances look to be at their worst, Your plan continues to unfold. For all along, You have the perfect strategy—the winning move. In Me, You have deposited grace into the so-called "game of life."

Jesus

DAY 35: A DAY IN THE DESERT

Do you believe God has a plan? Or, do you think He created things, set things into motion and now sits back in His regal chair watching the events of the world unfold? Are coincidences truly chance happenings, or are they evidence that God is acting in a remarkable, astonishing way?

Take the story of Esther, for example. Interestingly enough, the name of God is never mentioned throughout the entire book of Esther. Does this mean that God was not evident in Esther's situation? Were the circumstances surrounding her life just chance happenings, or was God involved?

I choose to believe that God placed Esther in the royal household; that He made a way for her to become queen so that she could be an instrument God used to protect the nation of Israel. When Queen Vashti was removed from her throne, King Xerxes searched the entire land for a beautiful, virgin to become the next queen. Out of all the women in the land, Esther was chosen; however, the king was unaware of the fact that she was a Jew. Haman, the king's highest official planned a conspiracy to kill all of the Jews, but his plan was thwarted when Mordecai (Esther's cousin) discovered Haman's evil plot. Mordecai reported his news to Esther and asked her to approach the king in order to stop Haman's plan to annihilate the Jews.

Read Esther 4:9-16. (For further study, read the book of Esther.)

Although Esther feared for her life, she did indeed approach the king, and Haman was eventually hanged on a gallows that he built for Mordecai's death. Interesting. Ironic. Coincidence? I think not.

Haman planned a terrible genocide, but God ended that plan. Was it a coincidence that Mordecai overheard Haman's plan to kill the Jews? Was it a coincidence that his cousin, Esther, was now in a position to influence the king? I think not.

Psalm 34 tells us that when we call out to God, He is there; when we realize our dependence on Him, He is there; when we spend time with Him, our faces shine; when we are brokenhearted, He is there.

Read Psalm 34.

If you believe that God's word is truth, then you have to embrace the fact that God really does care about us. He is an intimate, personal God who is concerned with every detail of our lives, and He will deliver the righteous. Although we may not see justice in this life, we can trust and believe that God will make everything right in due time. He does have a plan. His deeds are glorious and majestic, and we can trust in His righteousness which endures forever.

DAY 35: MY MOMENT IN THE WILDERNESS

Write a prayer or some thoughts about today's Day in the Desert.

DAY 36: MY WORD STANDS FOREVER

~ relax ~

GOD SPEAKS

My Child,

The grass withers and the flowers fall, but My Word stands forever.

God

DAY 36: A DAY IN THE DESERT

Flowers are beautiful. As my friend said the other day, "Flowers make me happy." I tend to agree with her.

We all know that flowers do not live forever. Their beauty only lasts for a moment. For that reason, each time my husband gives me a bouquet of flowers I take a picture. I also dry the flowers so that I can keep them for as long as possible. In fact, there are several dried flower arrangements throughout my house. Although these arrangements are beautiful, they pale in comparison to the original state of the flower. The vibrant color has dulled; the sweet smell of the rose is now non-existent. Quite frankly, some of the beauty has faded.

Life is beautiful, but we all know that we do not live in this human state forever. Our bodies grow old, weak and weary, and quite frankly, we begin to physically fade away. However, as Christians, when we grow in our faith our spirits only become more beautiful with each passing day. 2 Corinthians 4:16 says, *"Therefore, we do not lose heart. Though outwardly we are wasting away, yet inwardly we are being renewed day by day."*

Our spirits, our inward lives, need the word of God for renewal. We need to meditate on His truth day and night. God's word will never fade; the beauty of His promises will never die. We can rely on the faithfulness of God and His word, and that is why we do not lose heart. Our God is trustworthy.

Read the following verses:

Isaiah 40:8
Psalm 33:11
Psalm 119:89

Flowers fade. Physical life ends. The words of another person may not always hold true. But, God's word is firm; it stands; it is right and real! The question for us is this: Are we going to trust God? Will we take Him at His word, or will we hesitate? Are we brave enough to have faith?

Read Hebrews 11:1-3.

Sometimes it is hard to comprehend or believe that God exists; that Jesus overcame temptation in the wilderness; that Christ was raised from the dead. Sometimes it is hard to trust that our sins have been forgiven. It is hard to believe in something that cannot be seen, but that is where faith enters the picture.

Does the wind cease to exist simply because I cannot see it? No. Although I may not be able to see the wind, I can see its power. I may not be able to see the Holy Spirit of God, but when the pregnant teenager chooses adoption instead of abortion; when the husband allows his unfaithful wife to come home; when the addict puts the needle down for the last time; when lives are changed, restored and redeemed, I see the results of His movement; and those results strengthen my devotion to God. Through faith, the invisible becomes visible; crimson stains of sin become whiter than snow; the impossible becomes possible. Because of faith I hold to the conviction that I have a home in heaven. When my physical body gives way to death, my spiritual body will be in the presence of the Lord. I believe because I trust God's word, and He has made promises to me that I know He will keep.

How about you? What do you believe? How strong are your convictions? When the grass withers and the flowers fade, will your faith in God still stand?

DAY 36: MY MOMENT IN THE WILDERNESS

Write a prayer or some thoughts about today's Day in the Desert.

DAY 37: GOD OF RESURRECTION AND LIFE

SCRIPTURE

He himself bore our sins in his body on the tree, so that we might die to sins and live for righteousness, by his wounds you have been healed.

1 Peter 2:24

JESUS PRAYS

God of Resurrection and Life,

I sit beneath a tree today in desperate need of shade. The sunlight beams behind Me, and as it hits the tree branches the shadow of a cross is cast onto the desert floor. I stare at the cross, and I am reminded of My purpose in this place. For, I did not enter into the world to march into Jerusalem as a mighty warrior king. I did not clothe Myself with human skin in order to overthrow the powers of a corrupt government. I did not leave My place beside You to be seated on an earthly throne. Instead, I came to be lifted high on a cursed tree. I came to bring the forgiveness of sin and to give life. As I lean against this tree today and look upon the shadowy cross, I know that the Son of Man must be lifted up so that everyone who believes may have eternal life. For, I was not sent into the world to condemn the world, but to save the world. I know when My desert journey ends and I step from this wilderness into the city streets that I will be walking towards My place upon that tree. Yet, even still, I will obey You because it is when I am high and lifted up that Your name will be glorified.

Jesus

DAY 37: A DAY IN THE DESERT

Today I am facing my own personal test, for as I write these words, my father is lying in a hospital bed. In a matter of hours a doctor will inform us as to how we should treat a malignant mass found inside my father's body. Many of you understand the emotional strain because you have either been the patient, or you have waited at the bedside of a patient. Some of you are not strangers to the hustle and bustle of the hospital. Most of you are familiar with tubes, machines, monitors and medical jargon. All of us have been touched, in some way or another, by illness, disease and untimely death. None of us are immune to the troubles that come in this life. However, those of us who know Jesus Christ realize that we have hope in eternal life.

Read 1 Peter 2:24.

Christ was wounded and afflicted in His physical body so that we could be made alive. He healed our sinful hearts and gave us life. He was nailed to a tree because of our iniquities. We may not always experience healing for our physical, temporal bodies, but Christ has provided healing for our souls. Through faith in Him, we can experience life forevermore. I do not know if Jesus actually thought about His death, burial and resurrection while He was in the wilderness, but if Jesus did rest beneath a tree and see the shadow of a cross, I know He thought of you and me. You see, our sin led to a death sentence for Jesus Christ. When He chose to receive the penalty that we deserve for being unholy people, it meant that He would suffer and die for us. Because of the cross of Christ, we can have real life. Philippians 3:20-21 says:

> *But our citizenship is in heaven. And we eagerly await a Savior from there, the Lord Jesus Christ, who, by the power that enabled him to bring everything under his control, will transform our lowly bodies so that they will be like his glorious body.*

Will you join me in shouting "Hallelujah" to the Lord? We have hope because of Christ. Our bodies may be filled with disease, but one day they will be like "his glorious body." No matter what comes our way in this life, we can have peace because Jesus has given us the joy of salvation and the hope of eternity.

Read Philippians 4:4-7.

In times of uncertainty, remember the Lord is near. Rejoice. Do not be anxious. Allow God's peace to guard your heart and your mind—especially in times when you do not understand His reasoning or His ways. Regardless of the circumstances, God is worthy of honor, glory and praise! Soon doctors will advise us as to treatment for my father's physical ailment, but praise Jesus that the Great Physician has already healed my father's spiritual life. Because Jesus was lifted high on a tree, my father has a secure eternity. Do you? What is the spiritual prognosis in your life? Where, my friend, will you spend eternity?

DAY 37: MY MOMENT IN THE WILDERNESS

Is your eternity secure? Write a prayer or some thoughts about today's Day in the Desert.

DAY 38: BE STILL

GOD SPEAKS

Jesus,

B e still, and know…

I am God

DAY 38: A DAY IN THE DESERT

Does the great "unknown" ever unsettle you? I truly seem to function better in my daily circumstances when I have a schedule; when I have a plan; when I know what is going to happen next. I guess that is why I love a good mystery—because it is such a departure from my everyday life. I love suspense—when it is happening to a character in a book or a movie. But, when I am faced with uncertainty, I don't enjoy it quite so much.

I simply like to be in "the know." So, I would have to say that when my circumstances present me with open ended questions, I tend to get a little bit antsy. It is in those times that I have to remind myself that God's word tells me to be *"anxious for nothing"* (Philippians 4:6).

Read Psalm 46:10.

Do you ever stop to think that maybe our wilderness moments are God's attempt to get us quiet? If we hold to the idea that Jesus fasted for forty days, then for close to six weeks, He was without food. Although clear and alert in His mind, He may have not had very much physical energy; His movements may have been slower than usual. Quite possibly He could have been still; not striving; knowing full well that God is in control.

When the Holy Spirit leads us to the wilderness in our lives, maybe God is trying to slow us down, settle our hearts, clear our minds and allow us to be still so that we can know full well that God is in control.

Instead of wrestling with the great unknowns in life, instead of allowing the circumstances of our lives to cause us anxiety and to unsettle our faith, maybe we should take a step into the desert, get quiet, rid ourselves of any distractions and allow the Holy Spirit to minister to us.

Are you striving for answers instead of trusting God? Do you need to slow down and be still? Are you being led to a wilderness moment in your life? If so, don't be afraid to spend time in the desert; you will emerge from the wasteland fully satisfied in the Lord.

DAY 38: MY MOMENT IN THE WILDERNESS

Write a prayer or some thoughts about today's Day in the Desert.

DAY 39: MY SOVEREIGNTY

SCRIPTURE

Who let the wild donkey go free? Who untied his ropes? I gave him the wasteland as his home, the salt flats as his habitat.

Job 39:5-6

Rejoice greatly, O Daughter of Zion! Shout, Daughter of Jerusalem! See, your king comes to you, righteous and having salvation, gentle and riding on a donkey, on a colt, the foal of a donkey.

Zechariah 9:9

JESUS PRAYS

My Sovereignty,

This creature has been watching Me for weeks. I know she thinks I am strange. When I pray, it looks like I am speaking to Myself. And there are moments when she hears Me singing. To her, I am a rather peculiar Man; odd, yet inviting. She is curious about My purpose here. She wonders why I wander in the desert. I do not eat; she must wonder how much longer I can possibly survive.

When I walked into this wasteland habitat, she hid behind a hillside of rocks. She does not know that I have seen her; she has tried desperately to follow Me in secret. And yet, I am aware of her presence.

When I pray, she longs to hear what I am saying, but she is afraid to get too close. She is drawn to Me; as if a magnetic force is pulling her near. She approaches slowly, as if grazing, afraid that I will shoo her away. She clambers down among the rough terrain, her hoof slips; small rocks tumble towards the Me. She looks my way; fear in her eyes meet My gentle, yet piercing gaze. She senses an Almighty power around Me, and she is captivated.

I motion for her to come My way. She bows her head and tentatively moves closer. As she nears, I too approach. Standing now before Me, I can hear the rapid beating of her heart. Could she recognize My royalty? Does she know I am a King?

I caresses her head with a gentle hand and speak, *"Who let you go free, wild donkey? Who untied your ropes? I gave you the wasteland as your home, the salt flats as your habitat. You range the hills for pasture and search for any green thing"* (Job 39:5-6, 8).

She rubs her head into My hand, as if in response to My word.

I address her again, "Do you recognize Me donkey? Do you see Me like your ancestor saw the angel of the Lord years ago? Did you know Balaam's donkey actually spoke? O, the foolishness of such a man that God would use a beast to open his eyes; that a talking donkey would deliver wisdom. Such irony. Yet, beloved donkey, God often uses the unexpected and the absurd to get man's attention. For you, donkey, are such an instrument. As the prophet Zechariah spoke, *"Rejoice greatly, O Daughter of Zion! Shout, Daughter of Jerusalem! See, your king comes to you, righteous and having salvation, gentle and riding on a donkey, on a colt, the foal of a donkey"* (Zechariah 9:9). You see, there will come a day when I shall fulfill such prophecy; when I will enter into the city of Jerusalem riding upon a colt. Could it be your colt, dear one?"

The donkey knows I am the King; she knows the Messiah is in her midst for she humbly bows before Me, her knobby knees weak with awe for Me.

I sit upon the donkey's back! She has become My regal ride. I can feel her neck straighten as she holds her head high. She is carrying the Lord of Hosts, and I am celebrating as I say to her: "Oh, precious and humble creature, a day will come—not many years from now— when I will send my disciples into a village to find a donkey and her colt. For they shall be tied and My disciples shall loose them both and bring them to Me. And we shall make our triumphal entry into the city as the prophecy once spoken is fulfilled."

We prance around the desert floor as if dancing before a multitude of heavenly angels. I clap My hands and shout praises to the Lord God Almighty; My joyful laughter ringing out across the wilderness.

In the distance I hear another laugh, yet it seems to mock My parade of jubilation. At once the donkey ceases her prancing; struck with the wonder and the horror of the Lord's future entrance into Jerusalem. For upon her back rides the One who will be lifted up for all to see, both on a donkey and on the cross of Calvary.

Jesus

DAY 39: A DAY IN THE DESERT

One of my nieces is quite the girlie girl. At the age of eight, she asked me to take her to a clothes store so that she could try on outfits and model them for me. One night, when she was about four years old, I was babysitting. The time came for her to put on her pajamas and get into bed. When I went to tell her goodnight, I found her in a princess nightgown and a tiara. It truly was a picture-worthy moment. She is a queen in the making, and like most of us, she enjoys the "pomp and circumstance" of life.

The scene, however, was somewhat different for our Lord when He entered Jerusalem as king. Instead of the formal display of power and might, He entered with humility and peace.

Read Matthew 21:1-11.

I get so excited when I read how the life of Christ fulfilled the prophecies spoken of Him throughout the Old Testament. There is something so exhilarating about the truth being brought to light. The promised Messiah entered into the city on a humble donkey rather than on a war animal like the horse. Interestingly enough, 2 Samuel 18:9 and 1 Kings 1:33 tell us that King David and his sons used mules as their royal mounts. By riding on a donkey, Jesus, the Prince of Peace, was exemplifying His position in the royal line of David as well as His princely rule as the King of kings.

Unfortunately, most of us are unimpressed with lowliness; instead we want to rub shoulders with people of perceived wealth, power and prestige. We would rather follow the idea of a princess with a glass slipper and tiara than to settle for a meek and mild servant girl. We have been persuaded to believe that we deserve service. We refuse to accept the notion that we have been called to serve.

Jesus said in Matthew 20:26-28:

Whoever wants to become great among you must be your servant, and whoever wants to be first must be your slave—

just as the Son of Man did not come to be served, but to serve, and to give his life as a ransom for many.

Our world does not give accolades and rewards to people who clean toilets, wash sheets and make beds for us; sometimes they are the forgotten among us—especially in a world where money, position and power have such influence over us.

There is certainly nothing wrong with enjoying a fashion show or donning a tiara; it's when the lust for prestige and power overshadow the purity of serving others with our lives that we make "pomp and circumstance" frivolous and ridiculous.

My niece may indeed wear a crown someday; she may be in a worldly position of fame and fortune. However, my prayer is that she will always serve the Lord and that her life will echo the song of those who watched Jesus enter into Jerusalem on a donkey. I pray that all of us will forever bless the Lord as we proclaim "Hosanna in the highest!"

Are you wearing a frivolous crown today? Do you need to remove some of the "pomp and circumstance" from your life so that you can become a true servant to the people around you? Are you more interested in parading through life on wealth, fame and prominence, or are you ready to dismount from your life of pride and bow to the Servant who saved you?

DAY 39: MY MOMENT IN THE WILDERNESS

Write a prayer or some thoughts about today's Day in the Desert.

DAY 40: MY DEFENDER

SCRIPTURE

Be self-controlled and alert. Your enemy the devil prowls around like a roaring lion looking for someone to devour. Resist him, standing firm in the faith.

1 Peter 5:8-9a

JESUS PRAYS

My Defender,

Today, as I walked throughout this barren region, I came across My enemy. He was full of anger and pride and paced around the desert floor like a lion ready to pounce upon his prey. I happened upon him, and yet he did not notice My presence. As I shielded Myself behind a thorn bush, I heard him say these words:

What a mockery He makes of Himself. Is He mad? Riding around on a donkey as if He is a King. What ignorance! For I hold the keys to this kingdom. Does He think a lap around the desert on a donkey's backside makes Him majestic? What a foolish, ridiculous Man. If He would only surrender to my power, then He could ride upon such tremendous earthly success and riches. No one could possibly attain more wealth than He. Yet He wanders around in peasant garb foregoing meals and sustenance. Does He not know the banquet I can set before Him; a feast of arrogance, pride and greed unparalleled in all of the world. And yet He finds satisfaction in prayers, humility and loneliness. Why does He serve an invisible God who denies Him the regal robes befitting a king? Why is He content to wander in the desert heat—with only beasts to give him comfort. Does He not wish for a palace and scepter? Does He not lust for the throngs of people to worship at His feet and do His bidding? Why will He not renounce His Father and become my prince—my follower? Such power could be His in but a moment if He would just give way to my suggestions.

Yet I see the flaming swords of the ones sent here to protect Him. I recognize them from days of old; they are like the ones sent to protect the Garden of Eden. For, it is only their presence that keeps me at a distance from the parading king. For now they thwart my plan. But, I will wait in hopes that my day will come. I will plot and scheme until the opportune moment, and then I will dangle such delicious treats before that meal-starved Man. I will whet His appetite with all the powers of earth. And this ludicrous spectacle of kingly behavior with such a dumb beast will pale in comparison to the procession that He will experience when His natural, carnal needs are satiated.

And should He bow to me, God Himself will be defeated—for I will own the Son—and He will do my work on this earth. God can have His heaven and His angels, but I will take His chosen people. The Sojourner's time in the desert makes my work easy; when He is weak and tired I will approach Him—His human flesh will be His demise and my reward. The heavenly throne He left will remain empty for eternity because He will sit at my right hand. Instead of saving the souls of man, He will lead them into captivity. Instead of opening the eyes of the blind, He will shield them from Truth. And I will rule.

Father, I know My days in this desert are almost over; and yet, I must still endure the final testing as I face My tempter. Do not allow his desires to come to fruition. For I delight to do Your will, O God. And, I long to upstage this phony prince—for I am the Prince of Peace, and I shall not leave My throne in glory empty forever. For, I know My rightful place, and I shall return there when My work on earth is done. Protect Me. Defend Me. For Your Word is My life.

Jesus

DAY 40: A DAY IN THE DESERT

Do you ever stop to think about the fact that the same devil that tempted Jesus in the wilderness is the same devil who seeks to destroy our lives? We are doing battle with the same enemy who deceived Eve in the Garden. The interesting part about our entire struggle with sin is that we already know how to defeat the enemy, and yet, in our human frailty, we still surrender to temptation. Somewhere along the way, we have accepted lies about our heavenly Father, and rather than trusting Him and obeying Him, we choose to depend upon ourselves, someone or something else to meet our needs. We have been tricked into believing that God's ways are not satisfying, fulfilling or fun. For some of us, following God means that we have to give up a lifestyle of what we consider freedom. Ironically, the so-called freedom to which we cling is really a trap. We fool ourselves into believing that the chains binding us to drugs, premarital sex, vanity, drunkenness, gluttony, greed and pornography are lifelines to abundant life. However, our love affairs with the ways of this world—with the sin in our lives—rob us of the peace and joy the Lord longs to give His children.

Satan does not dangle a tantalizing lifestyle before you because he loves you and wants the best for you. He actually hates you, and he wants to do whatever he can to destroy anything God created. He will tease you. He will torment you. He will provoke you. But, he is simply trying to tear you down for his own gain.

Read 1 Peter 5:8-9a.

The Bible does not teach us that Satan is looking for a Christ follower to *"devour;"* instead we read that he is looking for *"someone to devour."* He does not care who you are. His main goal is to destroy lives. Sometimes we can be tricked into becoming mediocre Christians because we hear that Satan attacks people who are trying to love the Lord. We buy into the idea that if we believe in God, go to church every now and then, treat people with kindness that we will fall below Satan's radar and that he will leave us alone. We convince ourselves that if we don't get too serious about our relationship with God, then we won't be a target for the enemy. But, if we are sold out to Christ, then we think Satan homes in on us and we become more attractive to him.

It is true, when you stand on the side of the Savior, you become a menace to Satan. In fact, you become a real pain in the neck. He watches the way you live your life, and he really does not understand why you praise God in times of trials. He cannot fathom why you would place a tithe in an offering basket when you can use it to buy a bigger house, a better car or more clothes. He does not understand the heart of the believer because he disagrees and positions himself against everything that is good, right, trustworthy and loving.

But, make no mistake about it—every human being has a target on his back. Satan wants to destroy everyone. Do you really think that he ignores non-believers? Do you really believe that he only fights against Christ followers, and that those who do not have a relationship with Jesus are left alone?

Second Timothy 2:24-26 states:

> *And the Lord's servant must not quarrel; instead, he must be kind to everyone, able to teach, not resentful. Those who oppose him he must gently instruct, in the hope that God will grant them repentance leading them to a knowledge of the truth, and that they will come to their senses and escape from the trap of the devil, who has taken them captive to do his will.*

The *"trap of the devil"* has taken non-believers *"captive to do his will."* A man in captivity has no freedom. The alcoholic without Christ, is in captivity. The prostitute without Jesus, is living in chains. The adulterer who does not have a relationship with Jesus, is in his own private prison of pain. People without Jesus are tormented, taunted and destroyed. Satan does not leave them alone simply because they do not worship God. He wants to annihilate everyone because God's plan is to save everyone.

Satan destroys lives. He hinders Christ followers from abundant life through his deceit. He binds ungodly people in chains of dependency upon the things of this world, and they become addicted to sinful pursuits which will never satisfy.

Everyone suffers in this life at some time or another. For those called according to God's purpose, suffering is not in vain. For those captive to the will of the devil, suffering is a consequence of chasing after the wind. No one can hide under Satan's radar. If you are a human being you are in a battle with Satan. If you are a Christian you can win that battle. God has deposited His Holy Spirit inside of His children, and that power is the same power that raised Christ from the dead. Christ followers can overcome when they submit to God and resist the devil. The Bible tells us that when Christians stand firm in their faith and refuse to give in to Satan, he will flee (James 4:7).

Read Ephesians 6:10-18.

You can withstand the assault of the enemy.

Read Isaiah 59:12-17.

God's righteousness is His breastplate; just as we wear the breastplate of righteousness in our battle against Satan. We have been given everything we need to stand against the enemy.

Do you ever think about the fact that the same righteousness of Christ that stood against Satan in the wilderness is the same righteousness that covers our sin? Wow! We have a breastplate of righteousness because of the blood Christ Jesus shed on the cross for us, and through that righteousness we have the forgiveness of sin and the power to defeat our enemy. Who needs to hide under a radar when he has everything he needs to stand firm and win?

DAY 40: MY MOMENT IN THE WILDERNESS

Are you trying to hide under Satan's radar, or are you fitted with the breastplate of righteousness and ready to stand? Write a prayer or some thoughts about today's Day in the Desert.

DAY 41: THE HOLY WORD

SCRIPTURE

Jesus, full of the Holy Spirit, returned from the Jordan and was led by the Spirit in the desert, where for forty days he was tempted by the devil. He ate nothing during those days, and at the end of them he was hungry.

The devil said to him, "If you are the Son of God, tell this stone to become bread."

Jesus answered, "It is written: 'Man does not live on bread alone.'"

The devil led him up to a high place and showed him in an instant all the kingdoms of the world. And he said to him, "I will give you all their authority and splendor, for it has been given to me, and I can give it to anyone I want to. So if you worship me, it will all be yours."

Jesus answered, "It is written: 'Worship the Lord your God and serve him only.'"

The devil led him to Jerusalem and had him stand on the highest point of the temple. "If you are the Son of God," he said, "throw yourself down from here. For it is written:

'He will command his angels concerning you to guard you carefully; they will lift you up in their hands, so that you will not strike your foot against a stone.'"

Jesus answered, "It says: 'Do not put the Lord your God to the test.'"
When the devil had finished all this tempting he left him until an opportune time.
Luke 4:1-13

JESUS PRAYS

The Holy Word,

My tempter comes near to Me; believing that My lack of bodily nourishment will cause Me to crumble under his schemes. However, he sees not that My Spirit is greater than he. My quest is not for power or fame, nor am I clamoring for control. Why should I lust over that which already belongs to Me? I want nothing more than to satisfy the desires of Your heart and to bring Your plans to fruition; to thwart the jealous cravings of this meager opponent.

He taunts Me, but I do not look upon him. I remember the days when he was brightest among Your heavenly beings—how beautiful is he. Yet now, the darkness covers him; he is enveloped within his own passion for glory—an evil that cloaks him. He cannot fathom the doom that awaits him because his vision is skewed with thoughts of an earthly dominion. He tastes My death on his lips, and he is satisfied. His own quest for power drives him to overlook the Temple's restoration—for I will be rebuilt after three days. My tempter sees not the hand of God at work; he sees only what his heart longs to see—his enemy destroyed.

He wants Me, even now, to bow down and praise him; to pay homage to an earthly prince. He forgets that I am not the first Adam; but I am the Son of Man. I am the very essence of God; and he cannot cause My heart to turn against Myself.

He approaches Me and says, *"If you are the Son of God, tell this stone to become bread."*

I am so very hungry. My body aches for food and longs for sustenance, but I do not desire to do anything contrary to Your will for Me. I cling to Your Word as I say to him, *"It is written: 'Man does not live on bread alone.'"* For God, I live for You!

He is still not through with his taunting and tempting. I am weak in body, and yet he leads Me to a high pinnacle—to the pinnacle of the temple, and he shows Me the valley below as he says to Me, *"I will give you all their authority and splendor, for it has been given to me, and I can give it to anyone I want to. So if you worship me, it will all be yours."*

O, God, the tempter shows Me an easy way to own the world—a simple way to have dominion on this earth—and yet, I will only worship the One true God. For there are no other gods before Me. So, I respond to My enemy by saying, *"It is written: 'Worship the Lord your God and serve him only.'"*

Your Word deters him once again, although he is still not finished with Me yet. He tries to pervert Your Word. He tries to use it to cause My demise when he says:

If you are the Son of God, throw yourself down from here. For it is written:'He will command his angels concerning you to guard you carefully; they will lift you up in their hands, so that you will not strike your foot against a stone.'

I am standing on the highest point of the temple in Jerusalem. Should I step out and throw Myself from this place, I will be protected. Yet, I will not test You, Father. I will not demand that You prove Yourself God. So, I respond to My enemy with Your Holy Word, *"It says: 'Do not put the Lord your God to the test.'"*

He places no other temptation before Me, and I am finally rid of his presence—at least until another opportune time.

I fall on the desert floor before You God. For You have blessed Me with strength in the battle—and We have won.

Jesus

CONCLUSION

Imagine the scene—Jesus is kneeling in the desert. He is tired from lack of food, so He suffers physically. Yet His mental anguish is more acute and profound than His stomach pangs. He quotes scripture—reminding Himself of His position—for He is God. His heart aches for the comfort of heaven—His home; yet, He perseveres through His desert trial because of His enormous love for the world. Two angels flank Him as He kneels to pray. He sees them not but feels the presence of peace and protection. They stand guard over the Savior as He humbles Himself to pray. Listen in to what they say:

First angel:
Oh, that we could carry Him back to His rightful place in glory. For His suffering here is only a shadow of what is to come.

Second angel:
How precious is the sight of our Lord. How marvelous is His name.

First angel:
As He kneels to pray, His shoulders seem to sag with the weight of sin He must carry for the world.

Second angel:
> *Oh His matchless love. How vast His love for all people.*

First angel:
> *To watch Him weep for the lost—oh that I could tell mankind this story—that I could describe to him the scene I am now of witness. His body bent before God, sobbing for those who have no peace or hope in their lives.*

Second angel:
> *No one is greater than He. Holy is the Lord.*

First angel:
> *To brandish my sword and cut down the enemy—to end my Master's burden is my desire.*

Second angel:
> *Yet we will do the Father's bidding to stand guard and worship the King of kings. For the battle belongs to the Lord.*

First angel:
> *What a sight to behold. Do you see what I see?*

Second angel:
> *He rises from the ground—a muddy trail of tears on His dust-filled face.*

First angel:
> *Oh, He aims to fight—for His fists are clenched, His knuckles white.*

Second angel:
> *Look, as He raises His face towards the heavens—lifting His arms to glory. Do you feel the power—the might?*

First angel:

Oh, a battle cry like none I have ever heard before—
like a lion roaring throughout the jungle. I cannot stand
before this picture of strength.

Second angel:

Nor I—for I shall join you on my face in awe before the
Lord.

First angel:

Holy, holy, holy is the Lord God almighty.

Second angel:

Who was and is and is to come.

Imagine now the scene—two angels face down in the desert before a holy Lord—His arms raised in victory because He knows He is God!

Jesus has just suffered through a 40 day wilderness fast, faced the devil and overcome temptation with the powerful Word of God! How marvelous! How wonderful! How glorious! I can picture Him standing with fist clenched, arms raised to heaven. I see Him weak from hunger, yet full of God's power and might. I see Him victorious in the desert!

How do you picture Jesus?

I see Him angry at the temple; a voice of strength when He cast out demons; merciful with the harlot; bold with the woman at the well. I see Him gracious when He replaced the soldier's ear; brokenhearted in the Garden of Gethsemane. He is forceful with the Pharisees and Sadducees. He speaks truth seasoned in love. He gathers food and heals on the Sabbath. He spent all night praying. I see the Savior—the One who traded His glorious position in heaven to endure a wilderness journey, betrayal from family and friends and death on a cross. I see the King—the One to whom every knee shall bow and every tongue shall confess that He is Lord. I see love. I see sacrifice. I see God.

The Jesus we know and serve has a power beyond anything we have ever known—He conquered death—destroyed that which seeks to destroy so many. Jesus is humble in heart, but He is ferocious when facing a battle. He is a picture of gentleness and kindness; but He is also a mighty warrior. The enemy waged war against Him; Jesus fought for us and won! He is strong—stronger than your fears, illness and marital problems. He is more powerful than alcohol and methamphetamines. His greatness stretches beyond our own human limits. He is God Almighty! The Great I AM! The Maker of heaven and earth! The Savior of the world. Jesus!

If Jesus really did sound that battle cry in the wilderness, rest assured He did it out of love for you and me. He fought for your freedom and mine—freedom from sin and death. When you look into the truth of His power, can you stand? Or, like the angels, do you find yourself face down in the dusty desert of your life?

ABOUT THE AUTHOR
_____

Jodi Rae Bailey has served in ministry for over 20 years in the areas of youth, missions and women's ministry. She earned a Masters in Christian Education from Southwestern Baptist Theological Seminary. She holds an undergraduate degree from the University of Memphis in English with a Concentration in Creative Writing. Bailey has over 100 Christian and mission education articles and editorials published in *Challenge* magazine and *World Changers Express*. She has written *Nail it Down*, a pre-project study for World Changers and the *2000 January Youth Bible Study* for the North American Mission Board. Bailey also authored *Youth On Mission: Beyond Belief*, a 12 month missions curriculum for the Women's Missionary Union. Jodi Rae is married to her husband Shay. They reside in Clermont, Georgia and attend Lakewood Baptist Church in Gainesville, Georgia.

ABOUT JODI RAE MINISTRIES

In 2000, Jodi Rae wrote *In the Shade*, a retreat curriculum designed for girls and women. She is available to lead conferences or retreats in your area.

Jodi Rae Ministries, also creates personalized, graphic artwork prints called VerseArt, which help support the needs of her writing and retreat ministry.

VerseArt is a unique piece of art created especially for you. God created you in a unique and special way and wrapped you in His love. Likewise, each piece of VerseArt is unique because it bears your name, and each name is wrapped in the word of God. You simply provide a name and pick from one of the many designs on the website. VerseArt pieces make great gifts for any occasion—birthdays, weddings, anniversaries, new births and Christmas! Please visit *www.jodirae.net* for more information.

Printed in the United States
122698LV00003B/19-102/P